INTO THE DEEP

Into the Deep Street

SEVEN MODERN FRENCH POETS

1938–2008

Edited and translated by
Jennie Feldman and Stephen Romer

ANVIL PRESS POETRY

Published in 2009
by Anvil Press Poetry Ltd
Neptune House 70 Royal Hill London SE10 8RF
www.anvilpresspoetry.com

Selection and translations
copyright © Jennie Feldman and Stephen Romer 2009
Copyright and publisher details for the French texts
are given on page 335

This book is published with financial assistance
from Arts Council England

Designed and set in Monotype Ehrhardt by Anvil
Printed and bound in Great Britain
by Hobbs the Printers Ltd
ISBN 978 0 85646 416 4

A catalogue record for this book
is available from the British Library

Note

THIS BOOK grew out of conversations between the translators, when Jennie Feldman asked Stephen Romer for his thoughts on her idea of translating a group of modern French poets. It quickly became a joint project and the two poets decided that it would follow Stephen Romer's concept of the "lignée de Follain", which he explains in the introduction. The versions were written and revised collaboratively. The task of choosing texts and of producing initial English drafts was originally apportioned as follows: Stephen Romer – Jean Follain, Paul de Roux, Gilles Ortlieb; Jennie Feldman – Philippe Jaccottet, Jacques Réda, Guy Goffette. The poems by Henri Thomas were to be shared. As they agreed that Stephen Romer should be responsible for the main introduction and the headnotes to the poets, Jennie Feldman in the end took on some of his translations (the Follain prose and some de Roux) and gave more time to reworkings.

Both poets have overseen, commented on and revised each other's work to the extent that they bear joint responsibility for the translations, which are therefore "unsigned".

A word on the conventions used in this book. In extracts from prose books, non-contiguous selections are separated by a row of three dots. Asterisks are only used as in the original texts. In the titles or headings in the main text, book titles are italicized. Poems without titles in the original are given in the Contents with their first lines in square brackets; in the text these are printed in small capitals.

THE EDITOR

TABLE

JEAN FOLLAIN

Exister (1947)
Métaphysique	40
Enfantement	42
La brodeuse d'abeilles	44

Territoires (1953)
Félicité	46
Absence	48
Au pays	50

L'Épicerie de l'enfance (1938)
Journées	52

Territoires (1953)
Bienvenue	58
La glace	60
Vie	62
Poissons	64
L'œuf	66

L'Épicerie de l'enfance (1938)
De la cave au grenier: EXTRAIT	68

Territoires (1953)
Pensées d'octobre	72
La pomme rouge	74
Églogue	76
Le retour	78
Appel champêtre	80

L'Épicerie de l'enfance (1938)
La guerre	82

CONTENTS

Introduction BY STEPHEN ROMER 19
On the Translations BY JENNIE FELDMAN 33

JEAN FOLLAIN

Exister (1947)
Metaphysics 41
Childbirth 43
The Bee Embroiderer 45

Territoires (1953)
Bliss 47
Absence 49
In the Country 51

L'Épicerie de l'enfance (1938)
Long Days 53

Territoires (1953)
Welcome 59
The Mirror 61
Life 63
Fish 65
The Egg 67

L'Épicerie de l'enfance (1938)
From the Cellar to the Attic: EXTRACT 69

Territoires (1953)
Thoughts in October 73
The Red Apple 75
Eclogue 77
The Return 79
Country Call 81

L'Épicerie de l'enfance (1938)
The War 83

HENRI THOMAS

Travaux d'aveugle (1941)
Audides 90
Innocence 92

Signe de vie (1944)
Petit drame 94
Jeunesse 96
Le bout du rouleau 98

Le Monde absent (1944)
Grenier 100
Derniers beaux jours 102
Vaine muraille 104
[Dans mon souvenir je vois...] 106
[Cette rue... il était quatre heures du matin...] 108

Nul désordre (1950)
Vieille rage 110
Nul désordre 112

La Nuit de Londres (1956)
 III : J'aurais dû commencer... 114

Carnets 1934–1948 (2008)
 EXTRAITS 118

PHILIPPE JACCOTTET

Poésie 1946–1967 (1971)
Lettre du vingt-six juin 126

À la lumière d'hiver (1977)
[Oh mes amis d'un temps...] 128
[Sur tout cela...] 132

HENRI THOMAS

Travaux d'aveugle (1941)
Audides   91
Innocence   93

Signe de vie (1944)
Small Drama   95
Youth   97
End of His Tether   99

Le Monde absent (1944)
Attic   101
Last Fine Days   103
Vain Rampart   105
[Thinking back, what I see…]   107
[That street… it was four in the morning…]   109

Nul désordre (1950)
Old Rage   111
No Disarray   113

La Nuit de Londres (1956)
  III : I should have started…   115

Carnets 1934–1948 (2008)
  EXTRACTS   119

PHILIPPE JACCOTTET

Poésie 1946–1967 (1971)
Letter of 26 June   127

À la lumière d'hiver (1977)
[Oh friends from old times…]   129
[Over all this…]   133

Paysages avec figures absentes (1976)
Le pré de mai: EXTRAIT   134
Même lieu, autre moment: EXTRAIT   136

Pensées sous les nuages (1983)
Le mot joie: EXTRAIT   138

Tout n'est pas dit (1994)
Avant-printemps en Provence   144

Cahier de verdure (1990)
[Tard dans la nuit d'août…]   148

Après beaucoup d'années (1994)
Un lécythe   156
Dame étrusque   160

Et, néanmoins (2001)
Rouge-gorge: EXTRAIT   162

JACQUES RÉDA

Amen (1968)
Pluie du matin   168
Prière d'un passant   170

Récitatif (1970)
Lettre à Marie   172

Les Ruines de Paris (1977)
Déjà vers le fond traversé…   174

Hors les murs (1982)
Deux vues de Bercy   176
Deux vues de Plaisance   180

Un voyage aux sources de la Seine (1987)
EXTRAIT: À proprement parler, la Seine…   184

Paysages avec figures absentes (1976)

The May Meadow: EXTRACT   135
Same Place, Different Time: EXTRACT   137

Pensées sous les nuages (1983)

The Word Joy: EXTRACT   139

Tout n'est pas dit (1994)

Early Spring in Provence   145

Cahier de verdure (1990)

[Late into the August night...]   149

Après beaucoup d'années (1994)

A Lecythus   157
Etruscan Lady   161

Et, néanmoins (2001)

Redbreast: EXTRACT   163

JACQUES RÉDA

Amen (1968)

Morning Rain   169
Prayer of a Passer-by   171

Récitatif (1970)

Letter to Marie   173

Les Ruines de Paris (1977)

  In its depths now, criss-crossed...   175

Hors les murs (1982)

Two Views of Bercy   177
Two Views of Plaisance   181

Un voyage aux sources de la Seine (1987)

  EXTRACT: The Seine properly speaking...   185

Retour au calme (1989)

Pont des Arts 186
L'amour 188
La bicyclette 190

Le Sens de la marche (1990)

Les pommes de Jules Renard : EXTRAIT
    v. Sort imprévu de la deuxième pomme ... 192

La Liberté des rues (1997)

Reconnaissance 194

Moyens de transport (2000)

L'écluse 196
Le vertige 198

L'Adoption du système métrique (2004)

Tashi à quatre ans 200

PAUL DE ROUX

Poèmes de l'aube (1990)

La rue profonde 206
La pluie 208
Encore le froid 210

La Halte obscure (1993)

Impromptu 212
Une jeune fille 214
Les étourneaux 216
À la mémoire du peuplier noir 218

À la dérobée (2005)

Il y a un mois encore 220
Un regard 222
Rue Beautreillis 224
Les foins 226
À la table du fond 228

Retour au calme (1989)

Pont des Arts   187
Love   189
The Bicycle   191

Le Sens de la marche (1990)

The Apples of Jules Renard: EXTRACT
     v. Unexpected fate of the second apple   193

La Liberté des rues (1997)

Acknowledgement   195

Moyens de transport (2000)

The Lock   197
Vertigo   199

L'Adoption du système métrique (2004)

Tashi Aged Four   201

PAUL DE ROUX

Poèmes de l'aube (1990)

The Deep Street   207
The Rain   209
The Cold Again   211

La Halte obscure (1993)

Impromptu   213
A Girl   215
The Starlings   217
In Memory of the Black Poplar   219

À la dérobée (2005)

Only a Month Ago   221
A Gaze   223
Rue Beautreillis   225
Haystack   227
At the Far Table   229

La bâche   230
Till Eulenspiegel   232
De jour en jour   234

Au jour le jour, 3: Carnets 1985–89 (2002)
    EXTRAITS   236

GUY GOFFETTE

Éloge pour une cuisine de province (1988)
Crépuscule, 2   246
Crépuscule, 3   248
Crépuscule, 4   250
L'extrême été   252
[Les enfants qui glissent…]   254
Giacomo Leopardi   256
Césare Pavese, 2   258
La déchirure du ciel: IV   260

La Vie promise (1991)
Hors de portée   262
Février à vélo: EXTRAITS   264
La visite   268
Un peu d'or dans la boue: VII   270

Partance et autres lieux (2000)
    Partance: EXTRAITS   272

Un manteau de fortune (2001)
Variations sur une montée en tramway   278
Envoi   282

L'Adieu aux lisières (2007)
L'adieu   284

The Tarpaulin   231
Till Eulenspiegel   233
Day by Day   235

Au jour le jour, 3: Carnets 1985–89 (2002)
EXTRACTS   237

GUY GOFFETTE

Éloge pour une cuisine de province (1988)
At Dusk, 2   247
At Dusk, 3   249
At Dusk, 4   251
Deep into Summer   253
[The children who slip in ...]   255
Giacomo Leopardi   257
Césare Pavese, 2   259
The Gap Between Clouds: IV   261

La Vie promise (1991)
Out of Reach   263
February on a Bike: EXTRACTS   265
The Visit   269
A Speck of Gold in the Mud: VII   271

Partance et autres lieux (2000)
Partance: EXTRACTS   273

Un manteau de fortune (2001)
Variations on a Tram-Ride   279
Envoi   283

L'Adieu aux lisières (2007)
The Adieu   285

GILLES ORTLIEB

Place au cirque (2005)

Les mauvaises soirées   290
Un geste   292
Café de l'Usine   294
Février   296
[Petite ville aux reflets...]   298
[Neige à Thionville...]   300
[La brume a dissimulé la brume...]   302

Carnets de ronde (2004)
Déménager
    EXTRAIT: Du fond de ces semaines...   304

Meuse Métal, etc. (2005)
Ode (pour traverser les jours sans maugréer)   308
Tirés de la suite Décembres
    [Voici plusieurs jours...]   310
    [Décembre, mois entre tous malcommode...]   312
    [Veille de veille de Noël...]   314
    [Par la fenêtre...]   316
    [Arrière-cour en hiver...]   318
    [La saison se désincarcère...]   320

La Nuit de Moyeuvre (2000)
    Pour un portrait de Saxl: EXTRAITS   322

Sous le crible (2008)
    EXTRAITS   330

GILLES ORTLIEB

Place au cirque (2005)
Bad Evenings   291
The Act   293
Café de l'Usine   295
February   297
[Small town with its gleams…]   299
[Snow in Thionville…]   301
[The mist has concealed the mist…]   303

Carnets de ronde (2004)
Moving
  EXTRACT: Out of the depths of these weeks…   305

Meuse Métal, etc. (2005)
Ode (for getting through the days without grumbling) 309
From the sequence Decembers
  [For several days now…]   311
  [December, the month most awkward…]   313
  [Eve of Christmas Eve…]   315
  [Through the window…]   317
  [Back-yard in winter…]   319
  [Haltingly season unshackles itself…]   321

La Nuit de Moyeuvre (2000)
  Sketches for a Portrait of Saxl: EXTRACTS   323

Sous le crible (2008)
  EXTRACTS   331

A READING LIST OF TRANSLATIONS   333
ACKNOWLEDGEMENTS   335

Introduction

SOME WORDS of explanation are required at the start of this anthology, which gathers together seven French poets from three generations. The oldest, Jean Follain, was born in 1903, and the youngest, Gilles Ortlieb, in 1953. The original "hunch", and it is one that has become a conviction over the years, is that Follain in fact stands at the head of a line of poets who have, to a greater or lesser extent, recognized themselves in his work. For one thing, the seven represented here have all at various moments expressed their admiration for the poet, either in written form, or (among the living) in conversation. Henri Thomas has written of Follain as one of the poets "qui parle *d'autre chose*", rather than of himself. He admires him also as a poet extraordinarily free of rhetoric. Jacques Réda has remarked on Follain's magical art of contiguity, his ability to set a current running between objects in juxtaposition, in the absence of any single governing metaphor – indeed there are scarcely any metaphors in his work. Guy Goffette has penned a typically witty poem, in the Follain style, and incorporating titles from the Norman poet's collections, "Usage de Follain". Seen in these terms, of loyalty, and even fealty, this cluster with seven sides, this septagon, is in fact self-suggesting. Obviously it is not exclusive, and each of these poets belongs also to other clusters, and has undergone other influences. But for our purpose, which is to present a definite *lignée*, or filiation, of poets, and to follow one significant and relatively untrodden path through the labyrinthine ways of French poetry in the last century, it is a useful point to start.

One hallmark of this grouping is the fierce independence of each of these poets, since they would only warily acknowledge that they belonged to anything resembling a school, still less a *chapelle*. They are all, in the nice French sense of that word, fairly *sauvage*, which does not mean that they are sociopaths, or that they cannot, on occasion, be perfectly urbane. But the *sauvagerie* is there in the work, which is solitary in feeling, whether alone in a room, or on a train, or on a Parisian street. Several of them quote approvingly Rimbaud's celebrated *On ne part pas* ("no one ever leaves") – quite cognizant of the fact they are frequently in movement. Apart from the notable exception of Henri Thomas, who is the author of several novels, these poets remain for the most part in disjunctive dialogue with themselves, and it is remarkable that even Follain himself, so scrupulously impersonal in his aesthetics, acknowledges that a poet lacks *le don de l'ubiquité*, the gift of being omnipresent. But a reading of Henri Thomas's recently published *Carnets* shows clearly how this haunted and obsessive young man managed to distribute, among a whole cast of characters, his own compulsions. In Guy Goffette's prose text "Partance", the image of the poet writing in a dilapidated, immobilized caravan at the bottom of his own garden is a poignant *résumé* of a mental condition, of a self-consciousness that cannot escape itself. And as we shall see, it is in the effort to escape, and in what is for them almost a moral imperative to *turn outwards*, that these poets recognize each other. "Despair does not exist for a man who is walking", writes Jacques Réda in *Les Ruines de Paris*, and it might serve as a motto for the others gathered here. But he adds the important qualifier, "as long as he really walks, and does not engage in chatter with someone else, or in self-pity, or in showing off".

In the very particular universe of twentieth-century French literary criticism, it comes as no surprise then that these poets are variously grouped as – to use the jargon – "poets of the referent"; they are also "poets of the quotidian", to use the other inevitable, federating sobriquet. This is a peculiar shorthand which to be understood properly must suppose an acquaintance with the multitude of other options on offer, poets of the "stupefying image" that governed the Surrealists, or, closely related to it, of the Freudian Unconscious; or, in one reading of Mallarmé, the poets of the *signifiant*, defined by Roland Barthes as the "un-end of all possible relations" in a given piece of language, or by Umberto Eco as the "open work". These are alternatively known as the Textualists or the

Minimalists, not to forget the extreme position of the *Lettristes* – related to the Russian avant-garde poets of *Zaum* – who dismantle not only syntax, but phonemes, and who revel in neologism. The poets we are trying to "isolate" found and find little affinity with any of this. That said, when the "Retour au monde" – probably best translated by the return to the referent, or to the world "out there", and to the stone that Samuel Johnson kicked to disprove Bishop Berkeley – was announced, and finally established, when Jacques Réda took over the helm of the *Nouvelle Revue Française* in the nineteen-eighties – it had something of an embattled *avant-garde* about it. Indeed, the importance of Jacques Réda, as a pivotal figure here, is crucial. This "movement" was perceived in some circles as a return, however wary, to a form of expression that might be termed lyrical-descriptive (with any connotation of effusion or afflatus subtracted). It also heralded the return of something resembling a stable perceiving ego. In actual fact, of course, the world had never been away; it was there in the Normandy of Follain's childhood, with all its objects in place; it was there in the seedy hotel rooms and seething streets encountered by Henri Thomas; in the next generation, it was decidedly there, in the flora and fauna of Philippe Jaccottet's scrupulous notations from the Drôme, and in his near-contemporary Jacques Réda's early poems from the Moselle.

* * *

IT MAY BE helpful, in order further to characterize our poets, to refer to some categories invented and defined by one of the most clear-headed figures of the early Modernist avant-garde: Pierre Reverdy. He is a fascinating figure, and one that, along with Philippe Jaccottet, has been among the most attractive to the *monde anglo-saxon*, as the French are pleased to collectivize it. Although there seem to be superficial likenesses – Reverdy's poems contain apparently solid objects such as lamps, walls, curtains, windows – his approach, especially in his early "Cubist" poetics, contrasts radically with the poets gathered here. The solid objects in a Reverdy poem are in fact what he called *éléments purs*, stripped of their *enveloppe sentimentale*, and freed from any *réminiscence livresque*. In English, Reverdy's strictures would include the following: a poem must not be mimetic or anecdotal, it must not go into "useless" detail (do not number the streaks on the tulip), and it must not employ allusion or draw on the myth-kitty. Added to this is the vexed question of "purity", a notion that has haunted French poetry ever since Mallarmé divided the language into *ici, brut – là, essentiel*, followed by Paul Valéry's definition of poetry as a "language within a language". These prescriptions help us to see what a "return to the world" entailed, exactly: in most things, for the poets here, it meant *do exactly the opposite*, just as Follain, who claimed to "admire" Surrealism, turned away from it and did something quite different.

If by *enveloppe sentimentale* Reverdy means the "film of familiarity" that hides the object from us, then all our seven poets can refresh the vision. But they do, absolutely, *reinscribe* the poem into a recognizably empirical and perceptible world. In Follain's prose piece, "The War", the child is embraced by his father, on the morning he goes off to the front, and he recalls "a few drops of coffee laced with alcohol" on his father's "drooping moustache"; in Henri Thomas's "No Disarray", the poet recalls his young manhood in Paris, "Over the trees of the Luxembourg at sunset, the Eiffel tower / Could have been made of golden, dusty glass"; Philippe Jaccottet considers the poppies in a May meadow: "Red, red! It's not fire, certainly not blood. Much too cheerful, too slight for that." It is as if they intended to burn out the cliché, or to correct the cliché, by looking more closely. The city of Paris itself is one of the most *inscribed* places on the planet, but Jacques Réda sets out to explore it, and come to it fresh. Réda, like Follain and Thomas before him, remains in that sense the eternal provincial, the young man out of Balzac or Flaubert or Stendhal, encountering the *grande ville* for the first time. In his vision the city swoops into focus – "on the corner of rue de Vaugirard, a small butcher's shop" and then out again into a quasi-metaphysical realm, "all I am now is a memory wandering lost from street to street as far as the dazzle of bridges, among these passers-by the winter sun dreams up." Paul de Roux is the most contemplative of all, sitting most often at his table as dawn rises over the urban darkness. As a sedentary, holding down an office job, he can feel the most vulnerable and frustrated, a stranded Romantic with his forehead leaning against the (plate-glass) window, as the rain falls outside: "the wrench/ is being here and watching the rain/ stream down the tiles ...". Guy Goffette, altogether more reactive in temperament, gets on a bike in February to blow away the blues, and escape "that promised poem, // stopped short at the first line ...". As for Gilles Ortlieb, in his "Decembers", he casts a determinedly jaundiced eye on the clichés of the (dreaded) "festive season" and delivers his verdict on Christmas decorations in the street: "shards to snag the gaze, sharp-angled and wounding/ in the gravid dark, a kind of luminous barbed wire...".

Poésie pure, that elusive wraith, is likewise laid to rest by these poets. Reverdy had decreed that only certain objects, or elements, could gain admission to the poem, and they had to show their credentials at the door: cloud, sun, shadow, table, rain – such were the acceptable *réalités*. The Surrealists had of course introduced a whole panoply of phantasmagoric imagery into the language – just think of Breton's wife "whose teeth leave prints like the tracks of white mice over snow". So much so, indeed, that it gave poetry, as one dissident commented drily at the time, "a severe migraine". But the Surrealists are still in thrall to the Image, and the centre of their art is the analogy – simile and metaphor. The poets gathered here are metonymic, their poems are more an accretion, and an arrangement, of contiguous perceptions, which is why movement, whether peripatetic or *en wagon* is so attractive to them. This is less true of Follain, who manages to append the dimension of time, and of removal, into a mysteriously assembled collage: "Sometimes a window would open, like a wing, releasing a girl in a blouse with faded lace, her skin fresh in its glory ...", or "A child is born / in a broad landscape / half a century later / he's just a dead soldier" or the vision of Tintoretto's red apple which "in the chiaroscuro of museums" manages to "remain". What is noticeable about Jacques Réda, and the younger grouping, is the topographically specific nature of the work, and how it fairly bristles with place-names. Gilles Ortlieb, a frequent traveller from Paris to Luxembourg, where he works, especially delights in strange disharmonies, culled from the eastern reaches of the Lorraine, appetizing destinations displayed on a departure board: "Blettange, Florange, Gandrange, Tressange or Œutrange". These are the old steel towns with their disaffected furnaces and tall chimneys, and Ortlieb writes about and photographs them with the fervour of an archaeologist, just as he frequents their beleaguered bars and bistros with the curiosity, and the compassion, of a humane anthropologist. Ortlieb and Réda both put their trust implicitly in the music of the place-name, especially in the laconic humour that is generated when the *enveloppe sentimentale* of the ensign is belied by the unpromising nature of the establishment, *viz* the Luxembourgeois "*Coyote Girls* cabaret" with its "shows and entertainments a go-go", standing next door to a slimming boutique.

*　*　*

FLOUTING what is perhaps Reverdy's most perplexing decree, the ban on *réminiscence livresque*, these poets are variously allusive to books and writers, paintings and painters, music and musicians. Art and artefacts in general, as well as the experience of landscape and the city, form a crucial part of their hold on the world. Within the ambit of French poetry more generally, since Gautier and Baudelaire, there has been an active "substantial alliance" – to adapt a phrase of René Char – between poets and practitioners of the visual arts, and most of the poets represented here have dabbled in the art of ekphrasis. Apart from that reference to Tintoretto, Jean Follain mostly strays rarely, it is true, from the Norman fastness of his childhood, his *Canisy intérieur*, while Henri Thomas's allusions are almost entirely literary. Philippe Jaccottet is married to a painter, Anne-Marie, and his vision is informed by painting. In his prose-work *Paysages avec figures absentes*, he evokes the paintings of Arcadia, by painters of the Renaissance, by Claude Lorrain or Poussin – artists who invested the landscape with nymphs and shepherds, in turn revived by them from Antiquity. He remarks that in Poussin's "harmonized world", there was "room enough for gods and clouds, for nymphs and trees". But Jaccottet, a poet of the modern era, dissolves the classical figures into the Provençal landscape he sees before him, where they remain as traces, wisps, ideas. What Jaccottet frequently does is to compare natural phenomena to man-made artefact. In texts included here, poppies resemble "so many little flags barely attached to their poles", mulberry trees "have the look of harps set up for the Invisible" and the robin, memorably, "carries this sort of scarf whose colour is tamed fire". Among Guy Goffette's delicate, early poems are accounts of paintings – by Rembrandt, Goya or Utrillo – and he has written a study of Bonnard and of the rôle that his wife Marthe played in his painting (*Elle, par bonheur, et toujours nue*). Photography is also a source, and his "Variations on a Tram-Ride" included here, which records an instant of encounter in the city, is inspired by one of Lartigue's images. Paul de Roux, also, alludes to painters of all epochs, both in poetry and prose. Both he and Goffette come to painting not as art historians, but as poets, inhabiting the scene before them, and freely investing it with their own memory, and their own longings.

The same is true of their literary encounters – each poet has to hand the works of authors that have become indispensable to them, as comfort and resource. The small shelf that furnishes Guy Goffette's caravan contains the books, as he writes in a poem called "On the Shelf " – "that are forever open and at all times / In the sunny rooms of the memory". Goffette is the most self-consciously literary of the group, and the selection here includes some of his *Dilectures* – possibly translatable as his "reading delights" – on Leopardi or Cesare Pavese. Hailing originally from a rural area in the southernmost part of Belgium, known as the *Lorraine belge*, it is perhaps inevitable that Goffette should feel kinship with Rimbaud, another disenchanted country boy from an eastern province, and his *Charlestown Blues* (a riff on Charleville) are a brilliantly allusive homage to the great poet. But he has written passionately also in defence of Rimbaud's unhappy companion of some years, Verlaine, *pauvre Lélian*, both in poems and in prose. As Goffette's work has increased in range, confidence and virtuosity, his love of Auden has borne fruit, adding urbanity and an international range of allusion to his palette. He has invented, with Jacques Réda, an attractive brand of self-irony, that rare resource in recent French poetry, learned in part from another of his *dilectures*, Philip Larkin. It is also learned from Henri Thomas, whose *vers brûlants et moqueurs* he celebrates in his "Petit Chansonnier pour Monsieur Thomas".

The art of allusion, as the Anglo-American Modernists knew, can generate all kinds of contextual irony. Irony of this kind is everywhere implicit in Gilles Ortlieb's tender-laconic observations, whether of the environs of his Luxembourgeois "exile", or of his travels in search of the sun (he was born and lived his first ten years in Morocco) – to Marseille, to Greece, to Rimbaud's house in Harar, to Egypt. Ortlieb has increasingly acknowledged his sources, or rather his *phares*, his literary beacons, as in a text here, in which he battens down on a dreary December evening to read "some almost unheard-of / proser from Central Europe", or draws comfort, in some hotel room or other, from the unflagging pessimism of Cioran's philosophy. In prose works, he has written of exiles, whether internal or external (including a deeply-felt study of Baudelaire's last months in Brussels), and of a group of neglected writers he has called "orphans". Jacques Réda, something of a literary omnivore, has written prose appreciations of many figures, and in particular of his literary hero, Charles-Albert Cingria, the Swiss prose writer, whose texts read like uninterruptedly brilliant conversation, a mix of erudition, digression, expostulation – apparently on every subject under the sun. Réda shares his energy and his tenacious curiosity. In *Celle qui vient à pas légers*, Réda has also written learnedly on prosody – and his own adventures with the alexandrine is a literary chapter all in itself. Jaccottet's vast range, as translator from several languages, and more recently as anthologist, hardly needs stressing; remarkable, rather, is how scrupulously he keeps explicit allusion out of his poems (similar in this to Yves Bonnefoy, André du Bouchet or Jacques Dupin – poets with whom he is closely associated). Henri Thomas has written with empathy on another tortured and coruscating poet, Tristan Corbière. It is in such complex lines of allegiance, of fierce and private instants of recognition and appropriation, often discovered in odd corners, that true literary genealogies come to exist.

* * *

A WORD needs to be said about form, and in particular about our decision to include passages of prose from each poet. Since Baudelaire's great apology for the prose poem, in his preface to the *Petits poèmes en prose*, the form has become so popular among French poets, it is meaningless to seal it off in any systematic way from texts that are prosodically, or in line-length, more recognizably poems. The poets here seem to switch from one to the other rather as a musician might switch from a flute to a clarinet – or a saxophone in the case of Jacques Réda, who is a renowned authority on jazz. But we are also concerned to present that type of text, which is accorded so little place in the Anglo-Saxon tradition, known as the *carnet*, or the *cahier*. This is neither an ordinary diary, nor an intimate journal, nor a commonplace book, nor yet an impersonal collection of, say, observations of the natural world. It is the type of text that makes up what Reverdy called his *Journal de mon bord*, or his log-book: the day-by-day, and frequently the moment-by-moment notations, stray thoughts, descriptions, quotations, aphorisms, that are the raw material from which these writers can "spring out" their poems, or their prose poems. Paul de Roux has published four thick books of this kind and Gilles Ortlieb frequently constructs sequences from his ongoing notebooks. Of course, between the original notebooks and their published form, a great deal of excision and editing takes place, but Ortlieb has explained that the notebook and the poem spring out of the same material. It may be that the notebook entries, written down *en vrac*, retain that form, after selection and revision. Or it may be that a certain series of observations sets up a kind of magnetic current in the language, a centripetal force that might result in a free-standing poem, and it is then that the hard work of fashioning the language into the required shapeliness begins. In Ortlieb's case the highly worked "blocks" that make up the poems of *Meuse Métal, etc.* are not governed by traditional prosody, but rather by equality of line length, which makes for their complex internal rhythms, and a very particular disjunctive music.

Paul de Roux pours his material into the same vessel each time, a rather loose non-stanzaic unit, in which enjambement or line-ending seems less important than the working-out of the thought or the conflict in the space of the whole unit. Follain's instantly recognizable, immutable form is also the single, non-syllabic unit, though shorter and more sinewy than de Roux's. Philippe Jaccottet's books are most often made up of sinuous and richly-orchestrated prose reflections, counterpointed by the short, concentrated lines of his poems; though here again both forms spring from the same material. Of the seven, it is Thomas, Réda and Goffette who ring the changes more formally. Goffette dances about nimbly in Verlainian fashion, from formal sonnet to delicate *chansonette*, while in recent years Réda has written extensively in alexandrines, revitalizing the line with inventiveness and wit. The form is somewhat freer in his powerful first three books of poems (see Jennie Feldman's translations from these in *Treading Lightly*, Anvil Press, 2005). Réda's compacted, syntactically dazzling shorter texts, like those in *Les Ruines de Paris*, also take the prose poem in French to new heights. In every case, we have tried to give a sampler of each writer's characteristic formal choices – including a passage from Henri Thomas, novelist – and also, as far as possible, to scoop from different points, early, middle and late, in their *œuvre*.

* * *

A FEW remarks, to conclude, about our title, *Into the Deep Street*. With two significant exceptions, Jean Follain and Philippe Jaccottet, the city street is the place where the inner tension and outer vision of our poets seem chiefly to collide and crystallize. There is nothing especially new about this; ever since Baudelaire's definitive lines, "Fourmillante cité, cité pleine de rêves / Où le spectre en plein jour raccroche le passant!" poets have trawled the streets and dipped in and out of the crowd. They too have measured their melancholy against "palais neufs, échafaudages, blocs, / Vieux faubourgs ..." or been transfixed by a passing face in the "rue assourdissante". And perhaps none is more in the Baudelairean spirit, oscillating between exaltation and horror, than Henri Thomas. He in particular is a prey to sensual and erotic temptation – more even than Goffette, whose observations remain more playful in that domain. His strange, obsessive novel, *La Nuit de Londres*, is really one long monologue about the temptation to walk the street at night, which takes on the feel of a descent into hell, a kind of vastation, a self-shaming (the drive most often being sexual hunger and pursuit).

In Thomas two poles, or axes, constantly recur – the street, and what he calls the *observatoire moral* of his room. The room is the place of recollection, of reason, of writing; the street, of immediacy, of madness, of dissipation. In the crowds he feels, with a mixture of fear and desire, his own identity dissolving into the collective. In this, he recalls no one so much as the early Eliot: "You had such a vision of the street / As the street hardly understands", from *Preludes*, could serve as a gloss to Henri Thomas.

Baudelaire's *Tableaux parisiens* are foundational in that they provide the various responses of the poet to the street – from the nightmare vision of "Les sept vieillards" to the compassion provoked in the poet by the vision of "Les petites vieilles". If the street is the theatre of Henri Thomas's secret shame and private exaltation, then the spirit that animates Jacques Réda's apparently inextinguishable energy and curiosity, as he trawls the streets of the city and its environs, is very different in nature. It is clear that Réda's is at bottom a sanguine, even an exuberant personality, and that the depression that stalks all these poets in different degrees, is for him kept at bay by this apparently compulsive *flânerie*. Whether he is, in fact, really a *flâneur* is a moot point; the way in which he explores, say, the twenty *arrondissements* of Paris in turn, seems too energetic, and even epic, for the term. He is a writer capable both of close, empirical observation, and of finely-spun, often humorous, flights of metaphysical fancy. No description of Réda would be complete without mention of his Solex moped, which he has now replaced with a modern *vélo électrique*. His grandfather manufactured bicycles, and the occasional *vélo Réda* can still, apparently, be seen. His poem "The Bicycle", included here, is nothing less than an act of devotion. Comparable with this poem is Guy Goffette's delightful "February on a Bike", in which he defies his writer's block with the injunction "Pedal hard, and no thinking". Gilles Ortlieb also keeps two elegant bikes, one in Paris and the other in Luxembourg. Many of these texts find their origin in a pair of sharp eyes on a free-wheeling bicycle.

The street is by its very nature *diversement fréquentée*, as the *Guide Michelin*, with nice euphemism, used to describe the red-light district of Pigalle. It is where the people walk, multitudinous, heterogeneous and democratic. One thinks of the photographs of Cartier-Bresson or Robert Doisneau. It is also a theatre of *otherness* and *strangeness*, more in the unsettling vein of W. G. Sebald. For Réda and Ortlieb, endlessly attracted to the diversity of people and things, and resolutely outward in attitude, the street is their meat and drink. These two especially are practitioners of what Yves Bonnefoy has described as a kind of *herméneutique sur le vif*; roughly translated, they are decipherers of meaning on the hoof. For Paul de Roux, on the other hand, the street can seem a "fetid alley", peopled by automata on their way to and from offices, quite cut off from natural rhythms. In truth, though, each one in this group, at different times, is exalted or cast down, and all of them are solitaries. In a graphic manner which these poets would surely approve, the soldiers at Verdun described three degrees of depression, or *cafard* – the grey, the black, and worst of all, the green. Whatever the colour of their own *cafard*, the poets included here are at their most moving when the depressive backdrop, that obscure *inquiétude*, or *déchirure* is palpable, but kept in check, by a deep-rooted discretion. As Gilles Ortlieb puts it, in an aptly pugnacious aphorism, "le réel, éternel vainqueur aux points" – reality always wins on points.

STEPHEN ROMER

On the Translations

FRENCH POETRY has been described as traditionally "Platonic", based on abstractions and essences, while poetry in English, proceeding from that language's gritty amalgam, is more "Aristotelian" in its immediate grasp of surface texture and phenomena. According to this distinction, the seven French writers here – impelled as they are, above all, by the visual world around them – seem to be constitutionally fitter for the crossing into English than most of their compatriots in the field of poetry. Indeed, it is their remarkable alertness to nuances of perception that we, their translators, have sought to match in our attentiveness to the texts before us.

Translation begins with listening – *un travail d'écoute* (Pierre Leyris) – and in the preparation of this book, that process has been amplified by circumstance: two translators in different countries testing and fine-tuning their drafts out loud down the wires. Our aim might be characterized as trying to recreate in English something of the "acoustic inevitability" of the original. Certainly these translations, while shadowing the French as best they can, are intended as autonomous poems; the occasional small liberties we have taken were in the interests of such autonomy.

As discussed in the Introduction, these writers share a literary kinship that goes back to Jean Follain. But their individuality and versatility are striking. Most immediately apparent is the variable *shape* of their work on the page. As far as possible, this has been preserved in the English versions since it is no less intrinsic to the overall *tone* than other key variables such as diction, rhyme and metre. Gilles Ortlieb's poems of urban disenchantment (or reluctant enchantment), their long, folded sentences neatly packaged, are characteristically low-key and require an appropriately sober English diction. Hence the sardonic use of "merriment" in the last line of the poem that opens "Haltingly season unshackles itself from season". (In Paul de Roux's poems, on the other hand, any ironic overtones in the English translation would be quite out of character.) By contrast, the lyrical abstraction and *gravitas* that distinguish the work of Philippe Jaccottet, with single lines sometimes suspended in his expansive poems, may call into play the higher registers of English: "Clouds seated in God-like majesty" ("Late into the August night...").

Two of the seven poets represented here, Henri Thomas and Jacques Réda, make significant use of rhyme and fixed metre. In the turbulence that characterizes many of the poems by Thomas, there is the sense that he needs the stabilizing grace of rhyme and metre to hold together the "disarray [hanging] in the air". The phrase comes from an untitled poem beginning "Cette rue ... il était quatre heures ...". Here, the poem's traditional form – alexandrines (12 syllables) arranged in four rhyming quatrains – is no less integral to its *sense* than the anguished articulations. No question, then, that an English version should have elements of rhyme and metrical regularity. By the same token, the poem "Le bout du rouleau" ("End of His Tether") would lose much of its ruefully humorous tone without the jingle of even-paced rhyming couplets – the lines helpfully long enough for the translator to find plausible rhymes. On the other hand, some of Thomas's poems – such as "Grenier" ("Attic") with its rhymed, six-syllable lines – have such compact symmetries that in order to produce an English version with equivalent rhyme and metre, one would have to concoct something of a pastiche. An alternative strategy was to adopt a looser pattern of rhyme, half-rhyme and assonance, while staying close to the measure of the French.

On those occasions when Jacques Réda uses rhyme, the poetic circumstances are rather different. Rhyme is just one aspect – and arguably not the most conspicuous – of a striking musicality that derives to a large extent from the lines' internal sonorities. How can these survive the ordeal of being Englished? Special attention to cadencing no doubt helps. And here English has the handy acoustic asset of words ending in -*ing*, notably in the present continuous tense, which has no counterpart in French. Rather like the effect of pressing down a piano pedal, participles and gerunds can help enhance and sustain the resonance of the English line: "sinking without a sound beneath the weight of mist / and reappearing further off, but fainter" ("Pont des Arts"). Another example is the word "flowing" at the end of the poem by Paul de Roux that provides the title for this book: "send light flowing / round and into the deep street" (French: *faire passer / alentour la lumière dans la rue profonde*).

It is to be hoped that the reader who has only minimal French will nonetheless roam the left-hand pages of this book in all their strangeness. For the twin shocks of strangeness and recognition – often invoked as prerequisites for effective poetry – are no less vital, it may be argued, for a satisfying experience of poetry in translation. And just as all reading involves complicity in the creative process, so the reader, by consulting the French originals offered here, will become party to the ongoing – indeed, endless! – process of translation. For instance, only by referring to the French can it be known whether the English word "you" was originally conceived as *tu, vous* or *on*. In Guy Goffette's "Crépuscule" poems, the intimacy of *tu* in addressing his childhood self feels very different in French from the all-embracing *on* (literally, "one") in the exuberant "Février à vélo"; both, in English, become "you". On the other hand, in the poems of Jean Follain, who hardly ever uses the first-person *je, on* is often a kind of universalized personal perception – "In her arms you would have known..." ("The Bee Embroiderer"); "We love / the good wine ..." ("Thoughts in October") – which accords perfectly with the absence of syntactic demarcation in his short-lined, minimally punctuated poems. Coincidentally, two key words for all these poets, reflecting their preoccupation with the ephemeral, are identical in French and English: *moment* and *instant*.

The various perks that go with gender distinction are likewise lost in English, of course. The bicycle in Réda's "La bicyclette" has a fleet beauty that is somehow enhanced by its feminine aspect in French. Other examples abound, but it is Goffette's prose poem that offers the most sustained instance of a womanly feminine-gender object: the consoling intimacy offered by Partance makes it unthinkable to use anything but "she" when referring to the caravan (*la caravane*). The grammatical agreement between different parts of speech is a key factor in the intelligibility of long French sentences. One way of avoiding confusion in the English is to insert an occasional strategic colon or semicolon. Another is to corral between dashes words that belong to a single phrase or thought. Occasionally a new sentence is the only elegant, effective solution. On the whole, though, these translations attempt to adhere to the punctuation of the French.

Finally, a brief word on the marvellous French prefix *re-* (*repartir*, *reboire*) which conjures earlier instances of virtually any action. It's a trick that English performs rather more rarely, and the translator has to resort to adding "again" or "once more" – though these do, at least, offer the metrical options of iamb and spondee, respectively.

Keeping company with these poets has presented a challenge beyond the various technicalities of translation. For all of them, the act of writing is, or was, an act of faith – urgent and redeeming. In Paul de Roux's memorable image, words are "cold and heavy bricks" that you pile up in the hope, but not the certainty, of "metamorphosis", when each brick is "suddenly winged". It is tempting to borrow the image and think of translation as likewise aspiring to metamorphosis (an idea brilliantly explored by Charles Tomlinson). Meanwhile, in the *en face* format of this volume, the original poems and their versions will no doubt resume their mutual interrogations each time they are read.

JENNIE FELDMAN

Jean Follain

JEAN FOLLAIN was born in 1903 in the small town of Saint-Lô, a *sous-préfecture* in central Normandy. Holidays were spent in the neighbouring village of Canisy, and it was there, under the strict but benign tutelage of his grandparents (his grandfather was the village schoolteacher) that the boy experienced the sights and sounds which were to feed his entire *œuvre*. As Follain matured as a poet, he made it his project to preserve, as exactly as possible, this rural world, which was irremediably changed by the Great War and its aftermath. In 1924 Follain left his native Normandy to study law in Paris, which was thenceforth his home. It was there that he died, in 1971, run over by a car near the Place de la Concorde. Follain made his career at the bar, moved on to the *magistrature*, and finally ended up as an Assize Judge at Charleville. Meanwhile, from the moment of his arrival, he participated fully in the literary life of the capital. In 1928 he joined the *Sagesse* group where he met poets like André Salmon, Pierre Reverdy, Pierre Mac Orlan, Max Jacob, and the painters Georges Braque and André Masson. Early prose texts such as *L'Épicerie d'enfance* (1938) led to his first book from Gallimard, *Canisy* (1942). *Usage du temps*, his first collection of poems, followed in 1943, then *Exister* (1947) and another set of prose pieces, *Chef-lieu*, inspired by a visit to the charred ruins of Saint-Lô, which seemed to him to mark the definitive destruction of his childhood world. Further collections of prose and poetry followed, including *Territoires* (1953), *Tout instant* (1957), *Appareil de la terre* (1964), *D'après tout* (1967), *Espaces d'instants* (1971). He also wrote a biography of an ecclesiastic – Follain was fascinated by the rites and vestments of the Church – *Saint Jean-Marie Vianey, curé d'Ars* (1959) and a book on food and recipes, *La Table*, published posthumously in 1984. His diary, *Agendas 1926–1971*, came out in 1993, and reveal Jean Follain as a literary *mondain*, a brilliant conversationalist, gourmet and connoisseur.

Métaphysique

Quand ils l'aperçoivent
au fond des chaumières
ses mains soutenant
le bol à fleurs bleues
devant ses seins tendres
ils sentent l'ardeur
puis tout s'évapore
du décor fragile
pour laisser flotter
la seule odeur nue
de métaphysique.

Metaphysics

When they glimpse her
inside a cottage
her hands holding
the bowl with blue flowers
to her tender breasts
they feel the warmth
then all evaporates
from the delicate scene
leaving adrift only
the naked fragrance
of metaphysics.

Enfantement

L'enfant tremblait en elle
au milieu des tissus roses
des veines bleues
du fiel sombre.
On voyait à travers la ville
cette femme dont les yeux
avec tout son corps
exprimaient la résignation
aux épuisantes constructions
de la chair et du sang.

Childbirth

The child in her quivered
amid rosy tissues
and blue veins
of sombre bile.
You could see her through the town
this woman whose eyes
with her entire body
spoke of submission
to the exhausting constructions
of flesh and blood.

La brodeuse d'abeilles

Dans ses bras on eût connu
le goût d'être et de durer
elle brodait seule
les abeilles au manteau du Sacre
malgré les épingles piquées
à son noir corsage ajusté
elle demeurait
au cœur d'une beauté formelle
plus intense
les yeux fermés
après qu'on l'avait regardée.

The Bee Embroiderer

In her arms you would have known
the taste of being alive and lasting
she was alone embroidering
the bees on the Imperial Cloak
even with the pins stuck
into her tight black bodice
she lingered
at the heart of a formal beauty
all the more intensely
eyes closed
after watching her.

Félicité

La moindre fêlure
d'une vitre ou d'un bol
peut ramener la félicité d'un grand souvenir
les objets nus
montrant leur fine arête
étincellent d'un coup
au soleil
mais perdus dans la nuit
se gorgent aussi bien d'heures
longues
ou brèves.

Bliss

The slightest crack
in a pane or a bowl
can restore the bliss of some great memory
bare objects
showing their delicate edge
flash for an instant
in the sun
but lost in the night
will also fill up on hours
long
or short.

Absence

Le métal fond pour se marier à l'air
et la consolation
abandonne un homme
caressant l'encolure
d'un cheval de labour
qui regarde
un horizon au froid plumage.
On voit un filet de fumée
une feuille qui s'envole
seul l'homme est obligé de sentir la durée.

Absence

Metal melts to join with the air
and consolation
abandons a man
stroking the neck
of a plough-horse
who gazes
at the cold plumes of horizon.
There's a wisp of smoke
a leaf that flies away
only man is forced to feel the duration.

Au pays

Ils avaient décidé de s'en aller
au pays
où la même vieille femme
tricote sur le chemin
où la mère
secoue un peu l'enfant
lui disant à la fin des fins
te tairas-tu, te tairas-tu?
Puis dans le jeu à son amie
la fillette redit tu brûles
et l'autre cherche si longtemps
si tard – ô longue vie –
que bientôt les feuilles sont noires.

In the Country

They had decided to go
to the country
where the same old woman
knits by the road
where the mother
gives the child a shake saying
now for the very last time
will you be quiet, will you be quiet?
Then the little girl playing with her friend
keeps telling her you're getting warmer
and the other searches so long
so late – oh life so long –
that soon the leaves are black.

Journées

Acreté de ces longs jours où tombaient des ondées chaudes.

Un enfant aux joues de pomme mettait les doigts dans son nez près des animaux recrus.

Puis, le soleil séchait la pluie et recommençait à fondre sur les jardins. Dans les plus grands de ces jardins des hommes travaillaient. La bouteille de cidre était posée par terre contre le buis et bouchée d'un gros bouchon de liège; à l'ombre, les hommes buvaient toutes les heures. Ils se parlaient peu, les nuages de poussière s'élevaient sous les pas des chevaux qui, parfois, agacés par les piqûres des bêtes, se mettaient à caracoler sur la route, mais le soleil ne pulvérisait ni chevaux ni hommes.

Une femme passait qui, pour dire quelque chose sur le temps, prononçait «On s'en va en eau». Il était vrai que des gouttes de sueur perlaient sur son front, mais son corsage s'agrafait jusque sous le menton, fermé par des boutons de corozo.

Ô neige! Parfois, nous nous réveillions ébahis par une neige immaculée.

Le chat marquait exactement ses pattes sur cette neige. Des oiseaux durs et noirs volaient; on entendait des hennissements.

Dans ces froids, les piètres histoires où il était question d'enfants pauvres visités des fées passaient dans notre aveuglement surchargées d'arômes.

Aucun des paysans d'alentour n'eût consenti à glorifier la beauté des campagnes blanches, ils la sentaient pourtant et vibraient sourdement à la grandeur des éléments lorsqu'ils contaient les grands hivers et la hauteur qu'avait atteint la neige dans tel chemin de charroi.

Long Days

The pungency of those long days with their warm showers of rain.

A child with apple cheeks had his fingers in his nose, next to the worn-out animals.

Then the sun would dry the rain and resume its melting over the gardens. In the largest of these there were men at work. The bottle of cider lay propped against the box-tree, sealed with a huge cork; in the shade, the men were always drinking. They didn't talk much, clouds of dust rose from the hooves of the horses, which sometimes, maddened by insect bites, went clattering down the road, though the sun pulverized neither horses nor men.

A woman passing by declared, by way of comment on the weather: "It'll turn us all to puddles". Indeed, drops of sweat beaded her forehead, but her bodice was fastened up to the chin with buttons of ivory-nut.

O snow! Sometimes we would wake astounded by an immaculate snow-fall.

The cat printed its paws exactly onto that snow. Birds flew by hard and black; you could hear whinnying.

In those cold spells, wretched tales of poor children visited by fairies went by us in our blindness crammed with good smells.

None of the peasants thereabouts would have gone so far as to glorify the beauty of the white landscapes, yet they felt it, quietly thrilling at the grandeur of the elements when they told of the hard winters and how high the snow had reached on this or that cart track.

Un enfant, le long du chemin de boue durcie, revenait portant au creux du coude une bouteille dans la fragilité du soir, un soir gaulois où rien ne pouvait laisser croire que le ciel allait tomber sur la tête des hommes, mais où une étoile au ciel imposait d'indéracinables idées théologiques.

Parfois, une fenêtre s'ouvrait, comme une aile, livrant une jeune fille à la chemise aux dentelles flétries, à la peau fraîche et dans sa gloire. Les yeux qu'elle enchâssait dans son visage irrégulier du nez et des lèvres étaient bruns velours comme ces chenilles sur les grandes feuilles du matin.

Dans toutes les maisons éclatait sous des dehors de roses et de fange la beauté des métaux et des fibres.

La vieille dame était assise sur le rebord de l'âtre et ne disait pas un mot. Sa tête s'avançait un peu en avant, ses deux mains étaient posées sur ses genoux, une petite perle noire brillait comme de la houille dans sa vêture. On voyait passer par la fenêtre un troupeau. On avait, dans le cours de la journée, raconté qu'une meule avait pris feu toute seule.

Un long dialogue se déroulait entre la vieille dame et le silence et les objets qu'il enveloppait. À la lampe: «Je ne t'allumerai pas encore maintenant, tu dépenses trop».

Les abois du chien recommençaient.

Un reflet de la table cirée égarait les yeux. Une seconde l'odeur de la cire passait, s'immobilisait dans un tourbillon fin, très fin, et redescendait aux abîmes. Rien n'était plus beau lorsqu'à cette heure amortie on entendait le son, non point d'un seul mais de plusieurs tambours, un cirque ayant planté ses tentes dans le bourg.

Elle montait se coucher avec encore le goût du pain et de la viande. De grandes ombres dansaient sur les murs de chaux.

A child was coming back along the hard mud road with a bottle in the crook of his arm through the frailty of the evening, a Gallic evening where there was nothing to suggest the sky was about to fall on men's heads, but where one star in the sky dictated unshakeable theological notions.

Sometimes a window would open, like a wing, releasing a girl in a blouse with faded lace, her skin fresh in its glory. Her eyes, framed in a face with irregular nose and lips, were velvety brown like the caterpillars found on broad leaves in the morning.

In every house there glowed, beneath the roses and muck on the outside, the beauty of metals and fibres.

The old lady was sitting on the ledge by the hearth, not saying a word. Her head was thrust forward slightly, a small black pearl gleamed like coal amid her clothes. Through the window a flock of sheep could be seen going past. Someone had reported, in the course of the day, that a haystack had caught fire all by itself.

A lengthy dialogue was underway between the old lady and the silence and the objects it enveloped. To the lamp: "I'm not going to light you just yet, you spend far too much".

The dog's barking resumed.

A gleam off the polished table caught the eye. For a second, the smell of wax wafted, paused in a slight – the slightest – eddy and dropped back into the depths. Nothing was lovelier in that muted moment than to hear not just one but several drums, for a circus had put up its tents in the small town.

She would go up to bed with the lingering taste of bread and meat. Great shadows went dancing across the white-washed walls.

Journée, ô journée passée, et que d'animaux muets, point tutélaires, voués à la mort sans phrase, dépourvus d'ailes.

Le lendemain chacun criait de-ci, de-là, dans les coins et dans les jardins, recherchait les faits, bienfaits et méfaits d'une nuit. Il y aurait lieu d'examiner d'un air songeur les empreintes de pattes sur les plates-bandes entourées de petits buis. Parfois, une poule étranglée, un petit chien changé par un mal étrange et qu'il faudrait abattre crainte de la rage, seraient le bilan de la nuit, ou seulement un papillon jaune soufre tombé sur le sol.

À ce calme carrefour où des poules noires aux pattes poussiéreuses picorent, près de la fabrique petit à petit délaissée parce que trop loin des centres, l'auto des grands malfaiteurs anarchistes était passée aux environs de 1913 et personne alors ne l'avait vue. Une fille pleurait seule, vouée à un enchantement qui la torturait. Les carrés de linge suspendus dans les champs n'avaient pas eu le plus léger mouvement et l'enfant caché dans les herbes brûlées avait continué à lire le livre savoureux.

The day, O all the day gone by, and so many mute animals, nothing tutelary about them, destined to die without a word, wingless.

Next morning each would go crying this way and that, in the corners and in the gardens, looking for what had been done, for better or for worse, in the night. There was every reason to examine dreamily the paw-marks left on the flower-beds ringed by small box-trees. Sometimes the nightly yield would be a strangled hen, a little dog altered by some strange malady, which would have to be shot for fear of rabies, or just a sulphur-yellow butterfly fallen to the ground.

At this quiet crossroads, where black hens peck about on dusty feet near the factory that's falling into disuse so far from the centres, the car of the great anarchist villains had gone by around 1913 and no one had seen it at the time. A girl was sobbing alone, sworn to an enchantment that tortured her. Squares of linen hung in the fields had not moved in the slightest and the child hidden in the scorched grass had gone on reading his delectable book.

Bienvenue

Dans la ferme rechampie
c'est un jour soleilleux
que l'on attend l'étranger.
Vêtu de drap noir et fin
et coiffé du chapeau haut
il va pousser la barrière
et dire amis me voici.
L'âne broutant le chardon bleu
la jument en robe sombre
le porc buveur de lait maigre
le chien au front étoilé
le chat sensible aux orages
devant lui seront les mêmes
qu'en la dure Antiquité.

Welcome

At the freshly painted farm
it is a sunny day
to be waiting for the stranger.
Clad in thin black cloth
and wearing a top hat
he will push the gate
and say friends here I am.
The donkey grazing on blue thistles
the mare with a dark coat
the pig drinking thin milk
the dog with the starred forehead
the cat sensitive to storms
will be the same before him
as in hard Antiquity.

La glace

Après avoir monté les escaliers
de chêne sombre
elle se trouve devant la glace
au cadre que rongèrent les vers
elle y contemple un torse vierge
toute la campagne est embrasée
et doucement arrive à ses pieds
une bête domestique
comme pour rappeler
cette vie animale
qu'aussi bien recèle
un corps de femme.

The Mirror

Having mounted the stairs
of dark oak
she is there before the mirror
in its worm-eaten frame
she contemplates a virgin breast
the countryside all ablaze
and softly at her feet appears
a creature of the house
as if to recall
the animal life
a woman's body
can just as well conceal.

Vie

Il naît un enfant
dans un grand paysage
un demi-siècle après
il n'est qu'un soldat mort
et c'était là cet homme
que l'on vit apparaître
et puis poser par terre
tout un lourd sac de pommes
dont deux ou trois roulèrent
bruit parmi ceux d'un monde
où l'oiseau chantait
sur la pierre du seuil.

Life

A child is born
in a broad landscape
half a century later
he's just a dead soldier
and that was him
the man you saw
appear and set down
a heavy sackful of apples
two or three of them rolling out
a noise among those of a world
where the bird sang its song
on the stone threshold.

Poissons

Les poissons
vus par l'économie
sont abaissés par des mains éplucheuses
grattant l'écaille
scrutant l'œil mort
alors qu'au jardin ploient les tiges
et que l'air pur qui passe
par l'entrebâillement d'une fenêtre
flatte une femme qui se dévêt
et qui jamais n'a vu la mer.

Fish

Fish
viewed economically
are flattened by brisk hands
scraping the scales
scanning the dead eye
while in the garden stems are leaning
and pure air passing
through a half-open window
plays on a woman who is undressing
and who has never seen the sea.

L'œuf

La vieille dame essuie un œuf
avec son tablier d'usage
œuf couleur ivoire et lourd
que nul ne lui revendique
puis elle regarde l'automne
par la petite lucarne
et c'est comme un tableau fin
aux dimensions d'une image
rien n'y est
hors de saison
et l'œuf fragile
que dans sa paume elle tient
reste le seul objet neuf.

The Egg

The old woman wipes an egg
with her work apron
a heavy egg the colour of ivory
that no one else can claim
then she looks at the autumn
through the little skylight
and it's like a delicate picture
confined to a single image
there is nothing
out of season
and the fragile egg
she holds in her palm
is the one new thing.

De la cave au grenier

(EXTRAIT)

Dans la cave, l'odeur de fût montait glorieuse. Au plafond, s'affaissait la poutre à la vie longue en qui durait la fibre des chênes.

Une grande caisse de bois – ancienne caisse à barres de savon, portant des majuscules aux seuls pleins marqués – contenait les cendres pour la lessive; une autre, identique, la charbonnette.

On avait adapté à ces caisses des couvercles en planches raccordées, maintenus par des charnières grinçantes, et les couvercles, lorsqu'on les laissait retomber, produisaient un claquement mat, qui dans l'heure des ombres qui s'allongent, pouvait faire à peine frémir une fleurette dans la courette voisine.

La porte de la cave avait double-battant. Les mousses, les lichens et de fines végétations qui vivaient sur elle dans des crevasses, où du terreau, par l'accumulation des poussières, s'était sourdement formé, pouvaient laisser penser que cette porte vivait d'une vie d'arbre.

Dans une cahute attenante à la cave, les outils de jardin attendaient qu'on en use, et la même rouille qui dans un coin perdu mordait sans relâche une vieille chaîne de revenant, des clous divers dont ces petits en arceaux dits cavaliers, cette même rouille ne pouvait rien à la bêche luisante, ni au râteau ardent qu'un usage constant préservait.

Dans la courette voisine de la cave, une petite auge de granit demeurait toujours pleine d'une eau croupie, dans laquelle, au vif de l'été, on ne voyait que le reflet d'un pignon d'argile et d'un ciel bleu. Pourtant, la maîtresse du logis affirmait qu'avec un simple microscope de bazar on pouvait dans cette eau découvrir des bêtes bizarres, toute une faune à antennes, pattes, queues divisées.

From the Cellar to the Attic

(EXTRACT)

In the cellar the smell of casks rose gloriously. Across the ceiling the long-lived beam sagged, its oak fibres still holding.

A great wooden chest – an old chest once packed with bars of soap, bearing capital letters marked only on the down-strokes – contained ash for the laundry; another, exactly like it, had blackening.

These chests had been fitted with lids assembled from planks and held by creaking hinges, and when you let them drop they gave a dull smack that amid the lengthening shadows could send the slightest shiver through a floweret in the small neighbouring courtyard.

The cellar had a double door. Mosses, lichens and delicate flora living on it, in crevices where gathering dust had secretly turned to mould, gave the impression the door was living the life of a tree.

In a shed adjoining the cellar, garden tools waited to be used, and the rust that in a forgotten corner kept gnawing away at a ghostly old chain and assorted nails – including the hooped ones called *cavaliers* – could do nothing to the shiny spade or the gleaming rake preserved by continuous use.

In the little yard next to the cellar, a small granite trough was always brimming with stagnant water, and in it you saw, at the height of summer, only the reflection of a clay gable-end and a blue sky. Even so, the lady of the house declared that with a simple microscope from the bazaar you could find strange creatures in this water, a whole world of them, with antennae, legs and forked tails.

Aux grands hivers, l'eau gelait dans la petite auge de granit, l'on pouvait en retirer un splendide bloc de glace, au cœur sale, que léchait doucement après sa course le chien altéré.

In the coldest winters, the water in the little granite trough would freeze, and you could lift out a splendid block of ice with a dirty heart, which the dog, thirsty from running, would lick at his leisure.

Pensées d'octobre

On aime bien
ce grand vin
que l'on boit solitaire
quand le soir illumine les collines cuivrées
plus un chasseur n'ajuste
les gibiers de la plaine
les sœurs de nos amis
apparaissent plus belles
il y a pourtant menace de guerre
un insecte s'arrête
puis repart.

Thoughts in October

We love
the good wine
we drink alone
when evening lights up the copper hillsides
no game-hunter sets
his sights now on the plain
our friends' sisters
appear more beautiful
although there is a threat of war
an insect pauses
then moves on.

La pomme rouge

Le Tintoret peignit sa fille morte
il passait des voitures au loin
le peintre est mort à son tour
de longs rails aujourd'hui
corsettent la terre
et la cisèlent
la Renaissance résiste
dans le clair-obscur des musées
les voix muent
souvent même le silence
est comme épuisé
mais la pomme rouge demeure.

The Red Apple

Tintoretto painted his dead daughter
carriages were moving in the distance
the painter died in his turn
today long rails
girdle the earth
and carve it up
the Renaissance resists
in the chiaroscuro of museums
voices break
often even the silence
seems exhausted
but the red apple remains.

Églogue

Dans la maison refermée
il fixe un objet dans le soir
et joue à ce jeu d'exister
un fruit tremble
au fond du verger
des débris de modes pompeuses
où pendent les dentelles
des morts
flottent en épouvantail à l'arbre
que le vent fait gémir
mais sur un chêne foudroyé
l'oiseau n'a pas peur de chanter
un vieillard a posé sa main
à l'endroit d'un jeune cœur
voué à l'obéissance.

Eclogue

In the shuttered house
he fixes on an object in the evening
and plays at that game of existing
a fruit trembles
deep in the orchard
remnants of stylish fashions
hung with the lacework
of the dead
float a scarecrow in the tree
that groans in the wind
but on a blasted oak
the bird is not afraid to sing
an old man has placed his hand
upon a young heart
pledged to obedience.

Le retour

Entre une fillette pour réclamer son père
chez le marchand de vin
il sacre mais finalement suit
la silhouette pâle à la natte ouvragée
qui marche de l'avant
tournant parfois la tête
pour s'assurer qu'elle a bien sur ses pas
cet ivrogne las à la blouse glacée
et dont sourit l'épouse
le buste pris dans un corsage d'ombre.

The Return

In comes a little girl to claim her father
at the wine merchant's
he curses but in the end follows
the pale silhouette with the elaborate plait
who walks in front
now and then turning round
to make sure she's being trailed
by that weary drunk in the shiny smock
whose wife is smiling
bust clasped in a bodice of shadow.

Appel champêtre

Un morceau de pain
couvert de raisiné sombre
est le goûter du garçon assis
sur un mur d'éclatante argile
et ses pieds pendants sont chaussés
de brodequins cloutés de fer;
lorsqu'on l'appelle de loin
il ne répond pas aussitôt
la même voix
clamant alors plus fort son nom
à l'unique syllabe brève
trouble à peine le calme des îles.

Country Call

A chunk of bread
covered with dark jam
is the boy's afternoon treat
as he sits on a vivid clay wall
and his dangling feet are shod
in hobnailed ankle-boots;
when a distant voice calls him
he does not answer right away
the same voice
shouting even more loudly his name
with its one short syllable
barely ruffles the island calm.

La guerre

L'enfant de 1914 se souvient du fils de l'épicier de son village, celui qui faisait tant de parties de boules. Un des premiers jours d'août 1914, il avait traversé la place chauffée à blanc, dans l'uniforme des cuirassiers d'alors: torse étincelant, casque aux crins noirs, épaulettes rouges; il avait franchi les deux marches qui conduisaient à la porte vitrée de l'épicerie-mercerie et, alors que de partout on le regardait à travers les vitres, il avait appuyé sur le bec-de-cane; son visage était pâle et plus sombres ses mains éraillées au contact des têtes de clous qui étincelaient sur les caisses qu'on déchargeait pour la boutique.

Il était arrivé ainsi sous le ciel munificent pour dire au revoir à toute sa parenté. Depuis que la guerre était déclarée, il n'était point tombé une seule ondée, les vieilles douleurs de la paix avaient fui, mais fouines et blaireaux remuaient les mêmes feuilles.

Il tenait dans sa main la garde du sabre et les narines des enfants à sarrau noir happaient l'odeur du cuivre. Quels grands docteurs en noir devisaient à ce moment, quelles petites souris menaient la sarabande dans les buffets?

Il y en avait cependant des hommes qui chantaient, d'autres qui buvaient avec un regard de biais résigné.

Et ce même enfant se rappelait son père le jour de son départ pour la guerre avec un contingent de réservistes.

La veille, il était revenu à la maison avec l'uniforme bleu et prêt pour le départ du lendemain. Il n'avait que quelques heures qu'il paraissait soucieux de vivre simplement.

La vieille marchande était passée poussant sa voiture grise. La mère s'occupait aux fourneaux, le père alors était descendu dans la rue et dans un soir empli de la même grâce que tous les jours, il avait marchandé quelques fruits. Il avait, durant le repas, parlé comme à l'habitude, souhaité le bonsoir à l'enfant qu'on avait envoyé dans sa chambre tôt et

The War

The child of 1914 remembers the son of the village grocer, the one who used to play so many games of bowls. One day at the beginning of August 1914 he had crossed the white-hot square in the uniform of the cavalrymen of that time: sparkling braid, a helmet with black horsehair, red epaulettes; he had bounded up the two steps leading to the glass door of the grocery and general supplies shop, and with everyone watching him through the glass panes, he had pressed the door latch; his face was pale, his hands darker, roughened by the nail heads shining on the crates they were unpacking for the shop.

He had come by under the bountiful sky to say goodbye to all his kinsfolk. Since the declaration of war not a single rain-shower had fallen, the old sorrows of peacetime had vanished, but the stone-martens and badgers stirred the same leaves.

He kept the sword-hilt gripped in his hand, and the nostrils of black-smocked children caught the smell of copper. Which great black-clad scholars were chatting at that moment, what little mice were leading a saraband in the cupboards?

Even so, there were some men singing, others drinking with sidelong looks of resignation.

And that same child remembered his father the day he went off to war with a contingent of reservists.

The day before, he had come home with the blue uniform, ready for departure next morning. He had only a few hours and seemed anxious to live them simply.

The old tradeswoman had gone by pushing her grey barrow. The mother busied herself with the cooking-stove. The father had then gone down to the street and in an evening filled with grace as on all other days, he had bargained over some fruit. During the meal he had talked as

qui savait que ce soldat honnête devait partir aux lisières du petit matin.

L'enfant avait entendu le jardin s'endormir, les arbres frémir un peu, la maison se ramasser; le lendemain, éveillé par l'attente et l'angoisse, il avait vu venir à lui son père maladroit dans ses courroies mal habituées. Un peu de café arrosé d'alcool perlait à sa moustache tombante, son cœur à nu saignait, il avait demandé à l'enfant le pardon d'injustes colères, tout un amour incroyable était apparu; une heure plus tard un soleil d'hiver avait lui, mettant des clartés au plumage des oiseaux et aux baïonnettes des colonnes d'hommes: ils marchaient sur la route gelée.

usual, saying goodnight to the child who was sent to his room early and who knew the good soldier was going to leave with the approach of morning.

The child had heard the garden fall asleep, the trees quivering slightly, the house settling down; next day, woken by the waiting and the worry, he had seen his father come to him looking awkward in the unfamiliar straps. A few drops of coffee laced with alcohol hung on his drooping moustache, his naked heart was bleeding, he asked the child's forgiveness for unfair bouts of anger, an entire and incredible love coming to light; an hour later the winter sun had shone, putting bright touches on birds' plumage and the bayonets of columns of men: they were marching down the frozen road.

Henri Thomas

HENRI THOMAS was born in 1912 in the eastern town of Anglemont and grew up in the Vosges, where his father worked the land and his mother was the village schoolteacher. A brilliant pupil, Thomas won a scholarship to the Lycée Henri-IV in Paris, and studied for a place at the prestigious École Normale Supérieure. His failure to take the final exams, and the torments that accompanied this decision, form the basis of two of his novels. Having given up the chance of teaching literature, Thomas determined to become a writer, and his early years were dogged by self-doubt and financial hardship. A period of travel followed, and his first poems were published in *Mesures* in 1939. His first novel, *Le Seau à charbon*, a remarkably intense narrative that takes place in the closed universe of a boys' boarding school, was published by Gallimard in 1940. At this time, Henri Thomas enjoyed the friendship and patronage of Gide, and during the war years he became, briefly, the senior writer's secretary. His first collection of poems, *Travaux d'aveugle*, came out in 1941. Shortly after this, Thomas, already an accomplished novelist and poet, made his first translations from German (Goethe and Ernst Jünger), Russian (Pushkin) and English (Melville and Shakespeare's *Sonnets*). In 1946, Thomas moved to London, where he worked for the translation department of the BBC. His experience there, inward, intense and often lonely, was transcribed in his novel *La Nuit de Londres* (1956). Meanwhile, his collection of poems *Nul désordre* (1950) records a certain accommodation with the torments and desires that convulse the earlier poems. In 1958–60, Thomas was Visiting Professor in French Literature at Brandeis University in the US. Back in France, he continued his prolific writing career, adding to his novels and poetry collections a study of Corbière – *Tristan le dépossédé* (1978) – a poet he prized almost as highly as Rimbaud. Henri Thomas died in Paris in 1993.

Audides

Combien je t'aimais, lenteur,
prudent cheminement de l'âme dans la vie
qui est montagne, qui est nuage, qui est
lourde fumée, obscure boulangerie,
retraite du bétail vers les fermes, abois,
noirceur des granges, lampe errante
qu'on balance dans le foin sous les toiles d'araignées:
l'âme, comme elle, rayonnait
dans la connaissance du soir...
Le matin deviné par l'enclume, la roue,
les pigeons aux volets, quand le peu de tristesse
s'effaçait devant les monts convoqués à ma fenêtre
pour que j'admire, pour que j'adore
ce monde élevé dans la couleur bleue,
– ô paysage, tu n'étais pas très sûr,
ô mémoire, cité trahie,
je ne respire plus le vent qui t'amenait
l'odeur des soirs et la fraîcheur des matinées,
et le souffle versé sur les chemins poudreux,
roulant l'émotion des forêts, animant
tout ce qui sommeillait dans mon après-midi,
ô cité qui n'étais jamais close aux marées
des saisons, qui buvais longuement la patrie,
maintenant cité morte où mon poème est seul
avec l'étoile et l'insaisissable génie
qui jette ses feux et transperce
l'âme toujours ivre de vie.

Audides

How I loved you, slowness,
the soul's cautious winding through life
which is mountain, which is cloud, which is
dense smoke, shadowy bakery,
cattle going home to farms, dogs barking,
blackness of barns, lamp roaming
as it's swung in the hay under cobwebs:
the soul likewise radiant
being intimate with evening...
Morning signalled by the anvil, the wheel,
pigeons outside the shutters, the wisp of sadness
fading in the presence of hills summoned to my window
so that I can admire, can adore
this world lofted into the colour blue,
– O landscape, you weren't so sure,
O memory, jilted city,
what I breathe is no longer the wind that brought you
the scent of evening, morning's freshness,
and breezes that swirl down powdery lanes,
rolling the feel of forests, enlivening
all that drowsed in my afternoon,
O city who never shut yourself off from the tide
of seasons, who drank long draughts of home,
now a dead city where my poem is alone
with the star and the ungraspable spirit
that hurls its fires, transfixing
the soul forever drunk with life.

Innocence

Dans la rue
j'aime une blonde chevelure
dansant un peu sur les épaules
de la femme qui me précède.

Je ne sais quel est son visage,
à peine puis-je imaginer
les longues jambes, la douce emphase
de la hanche qu'une fourrure
entoure en ce beau jour d'hiver.

Mon bonheur est instantané,
Je n'ai besoin pour le cueillir
que d'un regard à la beauté.

Léger, tranquille, je parcours
dans la lumière délectable
la cité changeante des jours,

mon bonheur est couleur de fable.

Innocence

In the street
I've fallen for blond tresses
dancing a little on the shoulders
of the woman ahead of me.

I know nothing of her face,
can barely imagine
the long legs, the gently accented
hips enveloped in furs
this fine winter's day.

My happiness is instant,
and to pluck it I need only
gaze, just once, on beauty.

Airy, serene, I move through
a shifting cityscape of days
in delectable light,

mine is a fable-hued happiness.

Petit drame

Carnet jeté pendant la marche,
tous les copains passent dessus,
puis les mulets, les voiturettes,
le camion de la compagnie
et tout le poids du régiment.

Le carnet reste dans la boue,
informe et noir, des oiseaux viennent
piquer les crottins et l'avoine,
les flaques mirent sans espoir
le pâle novembre lorrain,

dans une grange, moi je pense
à tout avec indifférence.

Small Drama

A notebook tossed away on the march,
the lads all flatten it underfoot,
then the mules, the carts,
the company truck
the full weight of the regiment.

The notebook lies in the mud
black and formless, birds come down
to peck at oats and droppings,
the puddles reflect without illusion
a pale November in Lorraine

and in a barn I think
about everything, and shrug.

Jeunesse

Dans le quartier de l'Opéra
où des filles marquent le pas,
tournant de-ci, tournant de-là
leur col flexible et délicat

le jeune homme qui vint des champs
erre longtemps, longtemps, longtemps,
l'esprit perdu, le cœur battant,
sa maladresse le défend.

Il retourne à sa solitude,
à l'exil humble de l'étude,
chambre d'hôtel, inquiétude,
et ce poème qui t'élude

ô vil quartier de l'Opéra
où des filles marquaient le pas
tournant de-ci, tournant de-là
leur col flexible et délicat.

Youth

On the boulevards of the Opéra
where the girls pace up and down
turning this way, and turning that
their svelte and lovely necks

the young man up from the fields
wanders along and on and on
mind astray, heart like a drum,
he's stymied by his awkwardness.

Back he goes to his solitude
to the humble exile of study,
to the small hotel room, worry,
and this poem eluding you

O vile Opéra boulevards
where the girls went pacing up and down
turning this way, and turning that
their svelte and lovely necks.

Le bout du rouleau

Le poète muet, défait,
s'appuie au comptoir du café.

Ses poèmes sont loin de lui,
c'était hier qu'ils ont fleuri

quand la lumière environnait
d'un duvet d'or le moindre objet

maintenant nu dans la poussière
près des crachats, fils de misère.

L'œil bleu, l'œil bleu de la pensée,
l'œil bleu languit sous une taie.

Conjurer le malheur avec
des refrains, des airs de rebec,

(jamais rebec ne fut à lui),
c'est tout ce qu'il peut aujourd'hui.

End of His Tether

The poet is silent, and undone
at the café bar he's leaning on.

His poems, already far away,
had flowered only yesterday

when the downy golden light
wrapped each thing however slight

that now lies stripped and dust-defiled
where people spit, misfortune's child.

The eye, the blue blue eye of thought
has clouded to a glaucous blot.

Warding off an adverse luck
with ditties on a scraped rebeck,

(though no rebeck was ever his),
is all, for now, he manages.

Grenier

Odeur de la famille!
Que j'aille me cacher
au grenier qui m'habille
de poudreuse clarté!

Que l'hirondelle crie,
qu'un chat me vienne voir,
la lucarne est emplie
de ciel et de silence.

Ou si l'averse inonde
les tuiles murmurantes,
que j'entre dans un monde
tout protégé d'absence.

Charbon du crépuscule,
l'ange t'apporte, à moi!
J'entends le vent léger
qui marche sur le toit.

Attic

The smell of family things!
Let me go and hide
in the attic, dress up
in its powdery light!

Let the swallow cry
and a cat come to visit,
the skylight brimming
with silence and sky.

Or if a shower drenches
the murmuring tiles,
let me enter a world
sheltered by absence.

Charcoal dusk, the angel
brings you here to me!
I hear the wind lightly
walking on the roof.

Derniers beaux jours

Cristal de septembre,
fragile, embué
d'un souffle léger,

la prunelle est bleue
le long du sentier
confus de clarté,

paroles dorées
qu'une voix timide
prononce à l'orée

des bois vieillissants
donnez à ma vie
quelque ombre de sens.

Last Fine Days

September crystal,
fragile, misted
by a breath of wind,

blue iris of the eye
along the path
blurred by brightness,

golden words
that a shy voice
murmurs at the edge

of ageing woodlands,
give to my life
some shadow of sense.

Vaine muraille

Une jeune mère
une bête douce
s'assied près de moi,
me sourit, et je
souris, l'enfant dort.
Insondable joie
du printemps banal,
encore un peu, les marronniers seront en fleurs,
nous trois ensemble au fond du jour,
et combien d'autres...
Vaine muraille
de la personne
quand tu t'écroules
on est si bien
dans la lumière.

Vain Rampart

A young mother
a mild creature
sits beside me
smiling, and I
smile back, the child sleeps.
Unfathomable joy
of an ordinary spring,
in a while the chestnut trees will flower,
the three of us deep in the day,
and how many others...
Vain rampart
of the self
when you crumble
it feels so good
in the light.

Dans mon souvenir je vois
une rue assez tranquille,
le soleil sur un pavois
de nuages immobiles.

C'est Paris chaud sous l'ardoise
et frais sous les marronniers,
le tabac, l'ennui, la phrase,
et rôder pour oublier.

C'est Paris comme avant-guerre,
diverse y fut ma jeunesse,
ô fatigue, ô nuit de pierre,
et la soudaine allégresse...

Quelle chambre abandonnée
se souviendra des instants?
Il fait noir dans les années,
le Temps mange ses enfants.

Thinking back, what I see
is a rather tranquil street,
the sun across a bulwark
of never-moving clouds.

It's Paris hot beneath the tiles
and cool beneath the chestnuts,
tobacco, boredom, something said,
and wandering off to forget.

It's Paris before the war
where my patchy youth was spent,
O exhaustion, nights of stone,
and all of a sudden, delight ...

Where is the room, left behind,
that recollects those moments?
It is dark inside the years
and Time devours its own.

Cette rue... il était quatre heures du matin,
je me souviens de mes fatigues d'autrefois,
après l'amour, et ces querelles pour un rien
et ces sommeils cruels dans le lit trop étroit.

Qu'elle était belle, l'heure immense du regret,
celle du petit jour dans le désert des rues,
et l'espérance triste: oh, si cette aube était
la fontaine où reboire une force perdue...

Tout au bord de moi-même, ivre d'être si faible,
je voyais, à travers une vitre confuse,
mes jours, mes nuits, mes volontés qui sont des rêves
et le filet rompu des malheureuses ruses.

L'aigre bleuet voulait fleurir, mais empêché
de sommeil, ce n'était qu'une tache souffrante,
le désordre flottait, vague fatalité,
toute forme hésitait dans ses lignes tremblantes.

That street ... it was four in the morning,
I remember all the vexations I had
in the wake of love, quarrels over nothing,
those wretched nights in a too-narrow bed.

How lovely, that time of boundless longing
at daybreak, the no-man's-land of the street,
and the wistful hope: oh, if this day dawning
were a spring to refresh a wasted spirit ...

From my self's brink, groggy with my frailty,
I saw, through the blur of the window-panes,
my days, my nights, my unreal reverie,
the broken thread of my luckless plans.

The bitter cornflower, willing to bloom
but bleared with sleep, was a smudge of pain,
disarray hung in the air, like doom,
each shape doubting its quivering frame.

Vieille rage

Une colère de putain ivre,
Une colère à flanquer des gifles,
Une colère à faire sonner
Une tête contre une porte
Une chute dans l'enfance la plus hagarde,
Quand l'édredon monstrueux devenait dolmen nocturne
Et quand la pluie
Des nuits d'automne
Riait, roulait,
Dans la gouttière démolie.

Old Rage

Anger of a drunken whore,
Anger fit to slap a face,
Anger fit to smash
Someone's head against a door,
A plunging into childhood at its most haggard,
When the monstrous eiderdown darkened to a tombstone
And the rain
Of autumn nights
Rolled and snickered
In the wrecked gutter.

Nul désordre

Je descendais la rue Soufflot, quel âge avais-je, vingt-deux ans,
Sur les arbres du Luxembourg, la tour Eiffel au soleil couchant
Semblait faite de verre blond et poussiéreux,
Je ne recherche aucun détail, je crois revoir briller des yeux,
Qui j'ai rencontré m'apparaît, la scène profonde se rouvre,
Le soleil du soir me guide de la Contrescarpe au Louvre,
Les cafés s'allument, je ferme un livre,
Je sens le délice et le supplice de vivre,
Les lumières font partout des espaces magiques,
L'amour inconnu se montre dans cette rouge musique,
Et le silence, le désert de la chambre où je rentrais tard,
Cette lampe que j'avais, phare de tous les départs,
Rien n'a sombré, tout grandit jusqu'au miroir de décembre,
Sur l'avenir s'ouvre toujours l'ancienne chambre.

No Disarray

Going down rue Soufflot, how old was I, twenty-two,
Over the trees of the Luxembourg at sunset, the Eiffel tower
Could have been made of golden, dusty glass,
Not searching for details, I think I recognize shining eyes,
The one I met appears, the scene re-opening to its depths,
From La Contrescarpe to the Louvre the late sun guides me,
Cafés brighten, I close a book,
Feel the bliss and wretchedness of being alive,
All around lights set up enchanted spaces,
Untouched love is there in the red music,
And the silence, my desert room when I come back late,
The lamp I had, lighthouse to all leave-takings,
Nothing lost, everything lengthens towards December's
     mirror,
And opening onto the future, the room that was.

La Nuit de Londres

(EXTRAIT)

III

J'aurais dû commencer d'une façon plus raisonnée, oui, plus abstraite. En me jetant dans le détail d'une description, je perds l'avantage de ma situation présente, sans qu'elle soit changée pour autant. Je perds la distance, – et je reste isolé, ce qui est absurde, alors qu'il n'est pas absurde d'être isolé dans un observatoire. Mon statut de résident étranger dans cette ville n'est pas une fiction juridique; je connais des Français qui vivent ici depuis plus de dix ans; ils ont pris toutes les habitudes anglaises; c'est beaucoup, et ce n'est rien pour ce qui est d'une véritable assimilation. J'ai vu des cas de mimétisme poussés jusqu'à l'imitation d'un accent local. Mais pourquoi ce mimétisme, pour se cacher de quel ennemi? Cela ne faisait pas longtemps illusion, et peu importait, car il n'y avait pas grand-chose à protéger là. C'est peut-être ce vide personnel qui les obligeait au mimétisme: celui de mes collègues qui est mort à l'hôpital de Charing Cross l'hiver dernier imitait presque parfaitement le gentleman; nous l'avons vu maigrir et s'exténuer dans une tenue si impeccable qu'il eût été offensant de lui demander sérieusement des nouvelles de sa santé. Son plus proche collègue («un ami» pour la circonstance), a recueilli de l'hôpital un carnet *intime* où La Barre (c'était son nom, Florian La Barre), avait noté presque chaque jour, au cours du dernier mois, son poids, qui diminuait régulièrement; mais ce n'était pas tout: on y trouvait aussi, datant, je crois, du mois de novembre (il est mort en janvier), ces quelques mots: *Vivement le printemps!* Ainsi, du gentleman par mimétisme, il restait tout de même cette exclamation, ou ce gros soupir. Cela n'autorise pas à affirmer que son existence fut malheureuse autrement que par la maladie; je me souviens

La Nuit de Londres

(EXTRACT)

III

I should have started in a more reasoned, yes, in a more
abstract way. Launching like that into a detailed descrip-
tion, I have lost the advantage of my current situation,
without it changing meanwhile. I have lost distance, – and I
am left isolated, which is absurd, though there's nothing
absurd about being isolated in an observatory. My status as
foreign resident in this city is not a legal fiction; I know
French people who have lived here more than ten years;
they have picked up every English habit; and that's a lot,
but nothing compared to thoroughgoing assimilation. I've
seen acts of imitation taken as far as the adoption of a local
accent. But why this imitating, and what enemy are they
hiding from? The illusion didn't last long, and it hardly
mattered, for there wasn't much there to protect. Possibly it
is a personal void that impels them to such mimicry: the
colleague of mine who died at Charing Cross Hospital last
winter was an almost perfect imitation of the English
gentleman; we watched him grow thin and emaciated and
still so impeccably turned out it would have been insulting
to ask seriously after his health. His closest colleague (or,
for convenience here, "friend") retrieved from the hospital
an *intimate* diary in which La Barre (that was his name:
Florian La Barre) had noted down during the final month,
on an almost daily basis, his steadily falling weight. But
that was not all. Also found, and dating, I believe, from
November (he died in January) were the following words:
Roll on Spring! Thus, with the gentleman-by-imitation
gone, there nonetheless remained this exclamation, or deep
sigh. But that in itself does not give us the right to claim
that, his illness apart, his existence was an unhappy one;

de lui comme d'un monsieur très satisfait d'être tiré à quatre épingles. Et n'aurait-il eu, durant ses quinze années de travail à l'Agence, que le contentement qui naît de la routine, ce n'est pas rien, dans une ville où la routine est feutrée d'images qui peuvent donner à un homme, sans l'aide d'aucune conversation, le sentiment de participer à quelque chose de grandiose.

Quand je parlais de cet employé qui prend le bus, je ne songeais pas précisément à La Barre, mais c'est lui que j'aurais rencontré, en continuant dans cette direction. Dès lors à quoi bon l'observatoire? Après La Barre, je ne pouvais plus rencontrer que moi, je serais retombé sur moi, fatalement; car entre La Barre et moi, il n'y avait qu'une différence de degré; il gagnait davantage que moi, s'habillait mieux, sans comparaison, parlait mieux l'anglais, etc. Une fois rendu à moi-même j'étais refait, ç'aurait été comme avant: ruminations, angoisse, blocus de la fatigue, – le mur au fond de l'impasse et toutes ses gribouillures, mais rien de vrai. La preuve, cependant, que je n'étais pas retombé de mon observatoire, au moment où j'imaginais cette chute vers moi-même à travers l'ombre de mon collègue décédé, c'est précisément que je pouvais l'imaginer; si elle avait eu lieu, je ne m'en serais pas rendu compte, en tout cas pas de cette façon-là. [...]

I remember him as a man well pleased with his sartorial perfection. And if he had received, from his fifteen years working at the Agency, no more than the satisfaction born of routine, that is still considerable, in a city where routine is padded with images that can give a man, quite unaided by conversation, the feeling of taking part in something very grand.

When I spoke of the office worker who takes the bus, I wasn't thinking specifically of La Barre, but he is the man I would have met, continuing in that direction. So what was the point of the observatory? After La Barre, I could only encounter myself, I would be back with myself, inevitably. For between La Barre and myself there was only a difference of degree; he earned more than me, dressed better – no question – spoke English better, etc. And once restored to myself, I'd been duped, things were as before: rumination, anguish, the dead weight of fatigue – the wall at the end of the impasse with all its graffiti, but nothing true. Yet the proof that I had not fallen once again from my observatory, at the moment I imagined that very fall towards myself through the shadow of my dead colleague, is precisely the fact that I *could* imagine it; if there had been such a fall, I would not have realized it, or in any case not in that way.

[…]

Carnets 1934–1948

(EXTRAITS)

Lundi 12 octobre 1936

[Bibliothèque] Sainte-Geneviève.

À la même table que moi est assis ce personnage que j'ai toujours rencontré dans les cafés du Boul'Mich, depuis que je connais cette triste promenade de la fatigue qui mène de l'Observatoire à la Seine. Il est remarquable par sa chevelure rousse qui lui descend dans le dos et se divise sur chaque épaule, une part en venant se joindre à la barbe également inculte et rousse. Il peut avoir le col de sa chemise aussi crasseux qu'on veut, ça ne se verra pas. Avec son front ridé et ses traits gros, il serait majestueux dans une forêt. Tous les étudiants ont vu cette célébrité de leur quartier.

À un moment, il compulse un journal de Courses avec la gravité sévère qu'il a toujours. Tout à l'heure il s'absorbera dans une vaste « méthode éclectique de la langue chinoise ». Un des interminables cheveux roux est tombé sur la page, et brille au soleil qui descend de la grande fenêtre juste sur le bonhomme.

Je l'ai vu se moucher furtivement dans un bout de papier de soie. Influence de la Méthode chinoise?

Vendredi 31 juillet 1942

Je suis passé hier soir devant une glace de magasin, et c'est elle qui m'a sauvé en me situant à mes propres yeux dans le monde des passants, dans le tableau de cette soirée. Mal vêtu, chemise pas changée de plus d'une semaine, pas rasé, l'air fatigué, obsédé, même un peu hagard; et en s'approchant bien, on pouvait voir des cheveux gris à mes tempes. Tel était ce rôdeur. Sachez aussi qu'il est marié, qu'il traduit des livres qu'il n'aime pas, qu'il a des crises de

Carnets 1934–1948

(EXTRACTS)

Monday 12 October 1936

Sainte-Geneviève (Library)

Seated at the same table as me is that character I always meet in the cafés on the Boul'Mich, ever since I've been taking that sad and weary walk from the Observatoire to the Seine. He is remarkable for the red hair that flows down his back and runs over each shoulder, part of it joining his beard in front which is equally red and unkempt. His shirt collar could be as filthy as he liked, no one would ever see it. With his lined forehead and massive features, he would be majestic in a forest. All the students have seen this local celebrity.

One moment he's reading through a Racing paper with his usual sober severity. Then he'll be engrossed in a huge *Eclectic Manual of the Chinese Language*. A lock of his never-ending hair has fallen upon the page, and shines in the sunlight coming down from the big window right onto the fellow.

I have seen him wipe his nose furtively on a scrap of silky tissue. Influence of the Chinese Manual?

Friday 31 July 1942

Yesterday evening I walked past a shop window, and that is what saved me, by placing me in my own eyes within the world of passers-by, in the frame of the evening. Shabbily dressed, shirt unchanged for over a week, unshaven, looking tired, obsessed, rather haggard, even; getting closer, you could see the grey hairs at my temples. Such was this skulker. Note also that he is married, that he translates books he does not like, that he suffers crises of quite crushing

paresse anéantissantes, qu'il est sournois, que, que – etc. Je me suis rentré dans ma forme, et il en est résulté du calme et de la liberté. Ce sont là les expériences de la solitude; elles sont assez rares, mais je suis sûr qu'elles sont profondément vraies et valent mieux que le remue-ménage de vérités, d'espérances et d'encouragements mutuels des conversations. Deux êtres entre eux ont trop tendance à se maintenir dans leurs illusions respectives, ne serait-ce que par politesse, gentillesse. Il est difficile d'accepter que chacun se développe comme s'il était seul, mais c'est pourtant ce qu'il faudrait.

29 septembre 1946

C'est la rue qui est dangereuse pour moi. Mes projets s'y volatilisent en même temps que mes forces: la rue est tantôt, pour moi, surexcitante jusqu'à l'égarement, puis déprimante jusqu'à l'impuissance, et il me faut du temps pour reprendre des forces.

Combien de corps de filles je retrouverais, en suivant ma mémoire, au cours de ces dernières années, depuis la première fille, à l'époque du lycée? Combien de bordels où je suis entré et rentré! Et les hôtels, dont je changeais tout le temps: combien de portes où j'ai épié, regardé, jusqu'à ce que tout soit éteint et endormi? J'ai passé des jours et des nuits entières dans un tremblement de curiosité érotique continuel. Dix ans de ma vie se sont ainsi déchiquetés. La pensée du travail urgent et de la pauvreté était mon meilleur garde-fou.

laziness, that he is sly, and that – etc. I came to re-inhabit my own form, and the result was a feeling of calm and freedom. These are the experiences afforded by solitude; they are quite rare, but I'm sure they are profoundly true and worth more than the whole blather of truths, hopes and encouragements proffered mutually in conversation. When together, two beings are only too likely to confirm each other in their respective illusions, if only out of politeness, civility. It is hard to accept that people develop as though they were alone, yet that is what one must do.

29 September 1946

It is the street that I find dangerous. That is where my plans evaporate along with my strength: the street can arouse me to a frenzy, then leave me depressed and impotent, and I need time to recuperate.

How many girls' bodies would I find, if I followed my memory through these last years all the way back to the first girl, when I was at the lycée? How many brothels have I gone to and gone back to! And all the hotels, moving on from one to the next: how many doors have I spied at, watching till all was quiet and asleep? I have spent whole days and nights in an unremitting fever of erotic curiosity. Ten years of my life have been shredded in this way. The thought of urgent work to be done, and of poverty, has been my surest safety net.

Philippe Jaccottet

PHILIPPE JACCOTTET was born in 1925, in rural Moudon, Switzerland (*Suisse romande*) where his father worked as a vet. Educated in Lausanne, Jaccottet moved to Paris in 1946 and then, in 1953, to Grignan, a village in the Drôme, northern Provence. He has been based in Grignan ever since, and the surrounding countryside, with its view of Mont Ventoux, has become the central resource of his poetry and of his prose meditations. Jaccottet's writing career started in the wake of general devastation, and from the beginning his project was to re-ground being, starting with his own, and with it language, in the simplest and humblest manifestations of the natural world. This quest goes hand in hand with great culture and sophistication – Jaccottet's parallel career as a translator of, among others, Hölderlin, Rilke, Robert Musil, Leopardi and Ungaretti has nourished his own reflections. In the early Parisian years the young poet met Francis Ponge, who encouraged him, but also writers like Henri Thomas and Pierre Leyris who helped him find his particular register, and rein in any tendency to high-flown lyricism. Jaccottet first came to prominence with the publication of *L'Effraie* by Gallimard in 1953. It was followed by *L'Ignorant* (1958) and a prose book *La Promenade sous les arbres* (1957). The poet returns tirelessly to the task of describing the natural world, and at the same time records the voices that would tempt him to doubt the utility (and even the feasibility) of such a project. The experience of grief is at the centre of the great collections of his early maturity, *Leçons* (1969) and *Chants d'en bas* (1974). In the first two volumes of *La Semaison* (1963 and 1971) Jaccottet published what are essentially his *carnets*, a scattering of fragments, written spontaneously at odd moments, and unrevised. Ironically for a poet so wary of setting anything down, Jaccottet has amassed over the years a formidable body of work, which is constantly being added to – most recently by a volume of memoirs about his childhood in Switzerland, *Le Cours de la Broye* (2008).

Lettre du vingt-six juin

Que les oiseaux vous parlent désormais de notre vie.
Un homme en ferait trop d'histoires
et vous ne verriez plus à travers ses paroles
qu'une chambre de voyageur, une fenêtre
où la buée des larmes voile un bois brisé de pluie...

La nuit se fait. Vous entendez les voix sous les tilleuls:
la voix humaine brille comme au-dessus de la terre
Antarès qui est tantôt rouge et tantôt vert.

*

N'écoutez plus le bruit de nos soucis,
ne pensez plus à ce qui nous arrive,
oubliez même notre nom. Écoutez-nous parler
avec la voix du jour, et laissez seulement
briller le jour. Quand nous serons défaits de toute crainte,
quand la mort ne sera pour nous que transparence,
quand elle sera claire comme l'air des nuits d'été
et quand nous volerons portés par la légèreté
à travers tous ces illusoires murs que le vent pousse,
vous n'entendrez plus que le bruit de la rivière
qui coule derrière la forêt; et vous ne verrez plus
qu'étinceler des yeux de nuit...

*

Lorsque nous parlerons avec la voix du rossignol...

Letter of 26 June

From now let our life be told to you by birds.
A man would churn out too many tales
and all you'd see through his words would be
a traveller's lodgings, a window
where tears have misted a rain-shattered wood...

Night settles. You hear voices under the lime trees:
the human voice shines like the earthward beam
of Antares which is sometimes red, sometimes green.

*

Don't listen any more to the din of our worries,
don't think about what has happened to us,
forget our name, too. Listen as we speak
through the voice of day, and let there be only
daylight shining. When we come to be drained of all fear,
when death seems to us mere transparency,
when it is clear as the night air in summer
and we are carried by lightness, flying
through all these imagined walls the wind leans on,
all you will hear is the sound of the river
flowing behind the forest; all you will see
is night's eyes as they gleam...

*

When we shall speak with the voice of the nightingale...

Oh mes amis d'un temps, que devenons-nous,
notre sang pâlit, notre espérance est abrégée,
nous nous faisons prudents et avares,
vite essoufflés – vieux chiens de garde sans grand-chose
à garder ni à mordre –,
nous commençons à ressembler à nos pères…

N'y a-t-il donc aucun moyen de vaincre
ou au moins de ne pas être vaincu avant le temps?
Nous avons entendu grincer les gonds sombres de l'âge
le jour où pour la première fois
nous nous sommes surpris marchant la tête retournée
vers le passé, prêts à nous couronner de souvenirs…

N'y a-t-il pas d'autre chemin
que dépérir dans la sagesse radoteuse,
le labyrinthe des mensonges ou la peur vaine?

Un chemin qui ne soit ni imposture
comme les fards et les parfums du vieux beau,
ni le geignement de l'outil émoussé,
ni le bégaiement de l'aliéné qui n'a plus de voisin
qu'agressif, insomniaque et sans visage?

Si la vue du visible n'est plus soutenable, si
la beauté n'est vraiment plus pour nous
– le tremblement des lèvres écartant la robe –,
cherchons encore par-dessous,
cherchons plus loin, là où les mots se dérobent
et où nous mène, aveugle, on ne sait quelle ombre
ou quel chien couleur d'ombre, et patient.

Oh friends from old times, what have we become,
our blood turning pale, our hopes cut short,
we've taken up prudent, niggardly ways,
we're soon out of breath – old guard dogs without much
to guard or to bite –,
we're beginning to look like our fathers...

Is there really no way we might triumph
or not be trounced, at least, before time?
We heard age creaking on sombre hinges
the day we first happened
to catch ourselves walking with heads turned back
to the past, wreaths of memories ready as crowns...

Is there no other way
but to shrivel into the dotard's wisdom,
the maze of lies or the pointless fear?

A way that is not an imposture
like the tints and scents of the elderly beau,
nor the whine of the blunted instrument,
nor the stammer of the lunatic whose only neighbours
are aggressive, insomniac and faceless?

If seeing what is visible becomes unbearable, if
beauty is truly no longer for us
– lips trembling as the dress is parted –,
let us keep on searching below,
let us search further off, where words steal away
and we are led on by who knows what
blind shadow or shadow-hued dog, patiently.

S'il y a un passage, il ne peut pas être visible,
s'il y a une lampe, elle ne sera pas de celles
que portait la servante deux pas devant l'hôte
– et l'on voyait sa main devenir rose en préservant
la flamme, quand l'autre poussait la porte –,
s'il y a un mot de passe, ce ne peut être un mot
qu'il suffirait d'inscrire ici comme une clause d'assurance.

Cherchons plutôt hors de portée, ou par je ne sais quel geste,
quel bond ou quel oubli qui ne s'appelle plus
ni «chercher», ni «trouver»...

Oh amis devenus presque vieux et lointains,
j'essaie encore de ne pas me retourner sur mes traces
– *rappelle-toi le cormier, rappelle-toi l'aubépine*
brûlant pour la veillée de Pâques... et le cœur
de languir alors, de larmoyer sur de la cendre –,
j'essaie,

mais il y a presque trop
de poids du côté sombre où je nous vois descendre,
et redresser avec de l'invisible chaque jour,
qui le pourrait encore, qui l'a pu?

If there's a passage, it cannot be visible,
if there's a lamp, it will not be the sort
the maid would carry two paces ahead of the guest
– and you'd see her hand turning pink as it shielded
the flame, the other pushing the door –,
if there's a password, it cannot be a word
that, written here, would suffice as warranty.

Let us rather search beyond our reach, or through some
     gesture,
some leap or forgetting no longer called
"looking", or "finding" …

Oh my almost aged and distant friends,
I'm still trying not to turn back on my tracks
– *remember the sorb-tree, remember the hawthorn*
burning for Easter eve … when the heart
yearns, tearful over the ashes –,
I'm trying,

but there's almost too much
weight on the dark side where I see us descending,
and who can still set each day right
with what's invisible; who ever could?

Sur tout cela maintenant je voudrais
que descende la neige, lentement,
qu'elle se pose sur les choses tout au long du jour
– elle qui parle toujours à voix basse –
et qu'elle fasse le sommeil des graines,
d'être ainsi protégé, plus patient.

Et nous saurions que le soleil encore,
cependant, passe au-delà,
que, si elle se lasse, il redeviendra même un moment
visible, comme la bougie derrière son écran jauni.

Alors, je me ressouviendrais de ce visage
qui demeure, lui aussi, derrière
la lente chute des cristaux humides,
qui change, avec ses yeux limpides ou en larmes,
impatiemment fidèles ...
                              Et, caché par la neige,
de nouveau j'oserais louer leur clarté bleue.

Over all this I would like snow
to fall now, slowly,
settle on things the whole day long
– in a voice that's always an undertone –
and give the seeds their sleep
well sheltered, biding their time.

And meanwhile we would know the sun
is climbing still on the far side;
that it will briefly – if the snow slackens – slip back
into view, like a candle behind its yellowed screen.

And then I would think back to the face
that likewise lingers behind
the slow drift of damp crystals,
changeable, eyes clear or brimming,
impatient to be faithful...
                  And hidden by snow
I would dare to praise their blue light over again.

Le pré de mai

(EXTRAIT)

Longer le pré aujourd'hui m'encourage, m'égaie. C'est plein de coquelicots parmi les herbes folles.

Rouge, rouge! Ce n'est pas du feu, encore moins du sang. C'est bien trop gai, trop léger pour cela.

Ne dirait-on pas autant de petits drapeaux à peine attachés à leur hampe, de cocardes que peu de vent suffirait à faire envoler? ou de bouts de papier de soie jetés au vent pour vous convier à une fête, à la fête de mai?

Fête de l'herbe, fête des prés.

Mille rouges, dix mille, et du plus vif, tant ils sont brefs! Gaspillés pour la gloire de mai.

Toutes ces robes transparentes ou presque, mal agrafées, vite, vite! dimanche est court...

The May Meadow

(EXTRACT)

Walking by the meadow today heartens me, cheers me. It's full of poppies in among the wild grasses.

Red, red! It's not fire, certainly not blood. Much too cheerful, too slight for that.

Don't they look like so many little flags barely attached to their poles, cockades that a breath of wind might carry off? or bits of silk paper tossed to the wind to invite you to a fête, the festival of May?

A festival of grass, of meadows.

Reds by the thousand, ten thousand, all the more vivid for being short-lived! Squandered for the glory of May.

All these transparent – or almost – frocks, barely fastened, quick, quick! Sunday is soon over...

Même lieu, autre moment

(EXTRAIT)

Nul qui travaille ici. Tout le monde est dans les vignes que les rochers me cachent, on entend seulement des fragments des histoires qu'ils se lancent de rangée en rangée, quand ils se redressent. Et la maison fermée est vide, avec ses hangars d'où la paille déborde, son jardin confus, plein d'ombre, de buissons, de fleurs, où une enfance est cachée, qui rit ou pleure avec la même conviction, dans les chemins.

Au milieu du pré, trois mûriers côte à côte sont pareils à des harpes dressées pour les Invisibles, les Absents, et dont la voix aussi se dérobe. Ils sont là groupés telle une haute et fragile barrière, telles ces choses qui se trouvent sur un passage pour intervenir, pour transformer: barrière, écluse, tamis. Ils filtrent le vent ou le jour, on voit bien, en tout cas, cette ombre à leurs pieds qui s'amasse; et quelque jour, je percevrai le chant qui s'en dégage. Ainsi voudrais-je filtrer le temps jusqu'à ce que je n'en aie plus la force ou le courage, enraciné dans la terre colorée.

Same Place, Different Time

(EXTRACT)

Not a soul working here. Everyone is in the vineyards, though rocks are blocking my view and there's only the sound of their chitchat flying back and forth over the rows when they straighten up. And the closed house is empty, its barns spilling straw, its tangled garden full of shade and bushes and flowers, where a childhood is hidden away, laughing or crying with equal conviction along the paths.

Standing together in the middle of the meadow, three mulberry trees have the look of harps set up for the Invisible, Absent Ones, whose voices have also slipped away. There they are, like a tall, fragile barrier, like those things that stand in your way and hence intervene, transform: barrier, sluice-gate, sieve. They filter the wind or daylight – either way, you can see the shadow gathering at their foot; and some day I'll catch the song that rises from it. That is how I'd like to filter time, until I no longer have strength or heart, rooted in the vivid earth.

Le mot joie

(EXTRAIT)

Je suis comme quelqu'un qui creuse dans la brume
à la recherche de ce qui échappe à la brume
pour avoir entendu un peu plus loin des pas
et des paroles entre des passants échangées…

(Celui qui n'y voit plus très bien, qu'il se fie à l'enfant
pareille à l'églantier…
Il fait un pas dans le soleil de fin d'hiver
puis reprend souffle, risque encore un pas…

Il n'a jamais été vraiment attelé à nos jours
ni libre comme qui s'ébroue dans les prairies de l'air,
il est plutôt de la nature de la brume,
en quête du peu de chaleur qui la dissipe.)

The Word Joy

(EXTRACT)

I am like someone digging through mist
in search of what slips away from mist,
having heard footsteps just further on
and words exchanged by passers-by...

(If it grows harder to see what's there, trust the child
with her wild-rose look...
He takes a step in the late winter sun
then catches his breath, tries one more step...

He has never been truly hitched to our times
nor free as one who cavorts in meadows of air,
his ways are more like those of the mist,
seeking the little warmth that dispels it.)

Toute joie est très loin. Trop loin probablement déjà,
comme il se dit qu'il l'a toujours été, même enfant,
s'il se rappelle mieux le parfum d'une pivoine humide
effleurée alors du genou
que le visage de sa mère jeune
dans le jardin où le cormier tachait l'allée de rouge.

Lui qui ne va plus même jusqu'au fond de son jardin.

Tel le coureur à bout de forces
passe à celui qui le relaie un bâton de bois blanc,
mais sa main tient-elle rien encore à passer derrière lui,
nulle branche pour refleurir ou pour brûler?

All joy is very distant. Already too distant by now, no doubt,
as he himself has always been, he thinks, even young,
recalling the scent of a peony that once
brushed moist against his knee
better than the face of his young mother
in the garden where the sorb-tree stained the path red.

He who these days doesn't even go to the end of his garden.

The way a runner whose strength is spent
passes to the next man the relay's white-wood baton;
but is he left holding nothing to pass back,
no branch to reflower, or to burn?

L'aurais-je donc inventé, le pinceau du couchant
sur la toile rugueuse de la terre,
l'huile dorée du soir sur les prairies et sur les bois?

C'était pourtant comme la lampe sur la table avec le pain.

Rappelle-toi, au moment de perdre pied,
puise dans cette brume avec tes mains affaiblies,
recueille ce peu de paille pour litière à la souffrance,
là, au creux de ta main tachée:

cela pourrait briller dans la main
comme l'eau du temps.

So did I invent it, the sunset brush-stroke
across the rough canvas of earth,
evening's golden oil on meadows and woods?

Yet it was like the lamp on the table with the loaf.

Remember, whenever your foothold slips,
dredge this mist with your failing hands,
collect this bit of straw as a bedding for grief,
there, cupped in your mottled hand:

it might, in the hand, shine out
like the water of time.

Avant-printemps en Provence

Ailleurs, plus au nord, en hiver, la neige cache l'aridité du sol d'une couche un peu molle, aux ondulations trop douces, et d'un blanc qui m'a semblé toujours monotone et presque artificiel: une sorte de costume de satin. Ce qui est beau ici, au contraire, c'est de voir le paysage presque entier couleur de terre, les arbres eux-mêmes à peine plus roses ou plus gris que la terre, comme si l'on découvrait, avec ces sillons, ces herbes sèches, ces chemins, ces rocs, les fondations même du monde, quelque chose de solide et de simple comme le sol, une forte ossature, un monument de pierre immémorial dont les seuls ornements seraient des guirlandes de lierre comme incrustées dedans, d'un vert sombre comme celui de l'yeuse et du laurier. Pas de luxe, pas de superflu, pas de molletonnage, rien qui dissimule ou qui déforme: la terre seulement, d'où tout sort et où tout retombe.

Et dès la fin février, quelque chose de merveilleux commence au moment où la lumière s'adoucit progressivement contre les murs des maisons: sur les branches noires des amandiers, sur celles plus lisses et presque pourpres des pêchers pointe ici et là un peu de blanc, un peu de rose. Et le surprenant de cette apparition, c'est que ces teintes infiniment fraîches, ces fleurs fragiles, délicates entre toutes, surgissent précisément non pas dans une abondance, dans un nid de verdure, mais sur du bois que l'on dirait mort, au-dessus de ce sol couleur de poussière, à l'abri de ces murs de pierres; c'est-à-dire que l'on voit opposés les choses les plus frêles, les plus fines, et le décor le plus rude et pauvre. Ainsi, justement, sans doute, parce qu'elle se produit sur un fond aussi austère, il n'y a dans cette floraison rien de mièvre. Comment exprimer sans la trahir cette violence muette, légère? On dirait presque du feu, on aimerait presque dire qu'aux feux de vieilles feuilles

Early Spring in Provence

In other places in winter, further north, snow hides the ground's barrenness with a rather flaccid layer, its undulations too mellow, and of a whiteness that has always struck me as monotonous, almost artificial: a sort of satin outfit. What is lovely here, by contrast, is to see nearly all the landscape earth-coloured, even the trees barely pinker or greyer than earth, as if, with these tracks, these dried grasses, these roads, these rocks, you were tracing the very foundations of the world, something as solid and simple as the ground, a sturdy skeleton, an immemorial monument in stone, its only embellishment the seemingly inlaid garlands of ivy, their dark green like that of the holm-oak or laurel. No luxury, no excess, no cushioning, nothing that dissembles or distorts: earth alone, from which all emerges, and into which all will return.

And from the end of February, something marvellous begins as soon as the light starts to soften on the walls of houses: the black branches of the almond, the smoother almost purple ones of the peach, are tipped here and there with a touch of white, a touch of pink. And what is astonishing about their appearance is the fact that these infinitely fresh hues, these fragile flowers, the most delicate of all, come forth not from any abundance, no nest of greenery, but from wood that looks dead, above this dust-coloured soil, in the shelter of these stone walls; which is to say, you see the most frail and dainty of things against the harshest, barest backdrop. It is no doubt precisely because the setting is so austere, that this flowering has nothing mawkish about it. How to convey, without travesty, this mute, airy violence? You might almost call it fire, you'd almost like to say it is in response to fires in the old leaves on park roads that these trees turn a sudden pink, while others' whiteness communes with the last of the snow on distant mountain peaks...

dans les allées des jardins répondent ces arbres brusque-
ment roses, alors que la blancheur des autres dialogue avec
la dernière neige à la cime des montagnes éloignées...

Mais quel est ce besoin de dire les choses, au lieu de se
contenter de les regarder? D'où vient aux écrivains cette
manie de tout changer en mots, de ce qui les touche ou
retient leur attention? Ne serait-il pas plus sage de tailler,
de traiter ces arbres, avant que de les décrire? Mais l'un et
l'autre sont nécessaires. Autrefois, les hommes pensaient
que prononcer le vrai nom d'un dieu, c'était s'assurer tout
pouvoir sur lui: aussi les prêtres avaient-ils soin de le garder
pour eux. Il y avait une vérité profonde dans cette croyance.
Celui qui saisit un paysage, un moment, une lumière, avec
les mots convenables, les guérit au moins provisoirement
de cette maladie qu'ont toutes choses de se dissoudre, de
disparaître, de nous échapper. Où s'en vont tous ces
moments, ces vies, et notre vie? Un beau poème, une
phrase accomplie les gardent, les enferment, donnent une
forme à ce qui n'est qu'insaisissable fumée. Ainsi l'homme
croit-il, et sans se tromper complètement peut-être, qu'il
est un peu moins étranger au monde, un peu moins impuis-
sant devant les ruses brillantes du temps.

But why this urge to speak things, rather than make do with observing them? Where does it come from, this compulsion writers have to turn into words everything that touches them or holds their attention? Would it not be more sensible to prune and look after these trees, before describing them? But both the one and the other are necessary. Once men thought that uttering the true name of a god conferred full power over him: the priests were accordingly careful to keep it to themselves. There was a profound truth in this belief. Whoever seizes a landscape, a moment, a light, with suitable words, cures them – provisionally, at least – of this malady whereby everything dissolves, disappears, escapes us. Where do they go, all these moments, these lives, and our life? A beautiful poem, a well-wrought phrase keeps them, encloses them, gives shape to what is no more than vapour and cannot be grasped. In that way a person, without being entirely mistaken, perhaps, can believe he is somewhat less alien in the world, somewhat less helpless in the face of time's brilliant stratagems.

Tard dans la nuit d'août,
l'œil du Taureau devient rouge
comme s'il allait ensemencer la terre.

Il sait qu'on va l'abattre tôt ou tard,
et pas de vache au pacage
de ce côté-ci du ciel.

À quel brasier échappés, ces frelons?

Moi, quand mes pensées brûlent,
je sais pourquoi.

Late into the August night,
the eye of Taurus reddening
as if his seed were going to sow the earth.

He knows they'll slaughter him sooner or later,
and not a single cow in the pasture
this side of heaven.

What is the fire they've escaped, these hornets?

With me, when thoughts flare up
I know why.

Cette nuit,
un vent glacé fouette les astres;
on dirait
qu'eux aussi flambent plus avides.

Y aurait-il même pour eux
de l'impossible?

Nuages assis en majesté comme des dieux,

ourlés de pourpre s'ils vont vers la nuit.

Tonight,
an icy wind is lashing the stars;
it seems
their blazing forth is also keener.

Might there be, even for them,
an impossibility?

Clouds seated in god-like majesty,

hemmed with purple if night is where they are heading.

Orvet vif comme un filet d'eau,
plus vite dérobé qu'œillade,

orvet des lèvres fraîches.

Toutes ces bêtes
ou esprits invisibles

parce qu'on se rapproche de l'obscur.

Slow-worm brisk as a trickle of water,
vanishing quick as a wink,

slow-worm with cool lips.

All these creatures
or unseen spirits

because we are nearing the unknown.

Trop d'astres, cet été, Monsieur le Maître,
trop d'amis atterrés,
trop de rébus.

Je me sens devenir de plus en plus ignare
avec le temps
et finirai bientôt imbécile dans les ronciers.

Explique-toi enfin, Maître évasif!

Pour réponse, au bord du chemin:

séneçon, berce, chicorée.

Too many stars this summer, Sir,
too many friends struck down,
too many riddles.

I feel I'm growing more ignorant
all the time
and soon I'll end up a half-wit in the brambles.

So explain yourself, elusive Master!

By way of reply, from the roadside:

groundsel, hogweed, chicory.

Un lécythe

Il n'y a sur ce vase qu'une image à peine posée,
à peine une figure à déchiffrer:
«Jeune fille à la lyre».

Comme si une ombre avait marché sur de la neige
ou que le vague écho d'une parole
nous vînt à travers un rideau,
ou que l'on tînt quelqu'un comme une lyre dans ses bras.

Serait-ce, en ces parages misérables de la mort,
la plus cruelle image ou la plus douce à dévoiler
en inclinant le vase au-dessus des mains tachées?

Je crains qu'alors, nul leurre ne soit tolérable
et moins qu'aucun, la lyre entre des mains de femme
qui nous aura troublés et comblés si longtemps.

Je crois qu'il n'y aura pas d'autre remède
que, tous liens arrachés, quelque chose de pareil
à un surcroît de jour.

Quelque chose comme la main de la lune sur le front
ou moins encore: comme la vue d'une pomme
dans la cage brumeuse du pommier?
Quelque chose comme une pomme couleur de crépuscule
dans la coupe des draps?

Il vient ici un pas dont le battement monotone
dispersera ces mots comme des oiseaux effrayés
ou en fera des mouches autour de la tête assiégée,
pires que son approche.

A Lecythus

On this vase there's nothing but an image barely traced,
barely a figure to decipher:
"Girl with a lyre".

As if a shadow had walked on snow
or a word's vague echo
had reached us through a curtain,
or you held someone like a lyre in your arms.

In these wretched environs of death, is this
the cruellest image or the sweetest to be unveiled
tilting the vase over mottled hands?

That's when any lure, I fear, would be unbearable
and least of all, in a woman's hands, the lyre
that will have haunted us so long, overwhelming us.

I believe there will be no remedy
other than – all bonds ruptured – something akin
to an extra measure of day.

Something like the moon's hand on your forehead
or even less: like seeing an apple
in the misty cage of the apple tree?
Something like an apple whose colour is twilight
amid the folds of linen?

There's a footfall coming closer and its dull beat
will scatter these words like frightened sparrows
or make flies of them round the beleaguered head,
more dreadful than what's approaching.

C'est la colombe intrépide ici qu'il faut dénicher,
elle seule! mais qui de nous peut la héler,
qui sait encore son nom, si elle en a,
qui a des yeux encore pour en soutenir la vue?

This is where the fearless dove must be sought out,
none but her! yet which of us can call to her,
who still knows her name, if she has one,
who has eyes to take the sight of her still?

Dame étrusque

On la découvre à demi couchée
comme pour un repas
sur le recueil de ses propres cendres.

Elle tient dans la main un éventail
qui a la forme d'une feuille.

Tout cela, depuis des siècles, immobile,
une urne en terre, rose,
et autre chose encore
qui nous invite à un tendre respect:

un coffret, même pas très lourd
ni très solide,
comme on verrait une boîte à onguents
à l'effigie d'une beauté vivante
sur sa toilette; et, non loin, son miroir.

Celle-ci fut tout l'amour d'un homme
une saison de Toscane, ou une vie,
sous le même soleil qui éclaire encore nos pas.

Mais le miroir n'a plus rien à craindre de son souffle,
et l'éventail en forme de feuille
n'aura plus à cacher aucune rougeur de honte.
Elle a dû désapprendre ce qu'était la brise …

Que c'est étrange, néanmoins, ces images de mortes
qui éveillent encore une espèce vague d'amour
chez les ombres que nous sommes devenus!

Etruscan Lady

You discover her half-reclining
as if for a meal
on the heap of her own ashes.

In her hand she's holding a fan
shaped like a leaf.

All this, for centuries, unmoving,
an urn, rosy earthenware,
and something else besides
that elicits our tender respect:

a casket, not so heavy
nor very solid,
looking like a box of unguents
with the likeness of a living beauty
at her toilette; and, close by, her mirror.

Here she is, one man's all-embracing love
for a season in Tuscany, or a lifetime,
beneath that sun which still lights our steps.

But the mirror need no longer shrink from her breath,
and the leaf-shaped fan
won't have to hide any chastened blush.
She must have unlearned what a breeze was…

And yet how strange, these womanly images of death
that still stir a vague sort of love
in the shadows we have become!

Rouge-gorge

(EXTRAIT)

Travaillant au jardin, je vois soudain, à deux pas, un rouge-gorge; on dirait qu'il veut vous parler, au moins vous tenir compagnie: minuscule piéton, victime toute désignée des chats. Comment montrer la couleur de sa gorge? Couleur moins proche du rose, ou du pourpre, ou du rouge sang, que du rouge brique; si ce mot n'évoquait une idée de mur, de pierre même, un bruit de pierre cassante, qu'il faut oublier au profit de ce qu'il évoquerait aussi de feu apprivoisé, de reflet du feu; couleur que l'on dirait comme amicale, sans plus rien de ce que le rouge peut avoir de brûlant, de cruel, de guerrier ou de triomphant. L'oiseau porte dans son plumage, qui est couleur de la terre sur laquelle il aime tant à marcher, cette sorte de foulard couleur de feu apprivoisé, couleur de ciel au couchant. Ce n'est presque rien, comme cet oiseau n'est presque rien, et cet instant, et ces tâches, et ces paroles. À peine une braise qui sautillerait, ou un petit porte-drapeau, messager sans vrai message: l'étrangeté insondable des couleurs. Cela ne pèserait presque rien, même dans une main d'enfant.

Cependant vous parvient aux oreilles, par intermittence, le bruit discret, comme prudent, des dernières feuilles du figuier; celui, plus ample mais plus lointain, des hauts platanes d'un parc; c'est la rumeur du vent invisible, le bruit de l'invisible. À l'abri duquel le rouge-gorge et moi vaquons à nos besognes. Lui, le porte-lanterne, l'imprudent, si rôde un chat.

Redbreast

(EXTRACT)

Working in the garden, all of a sudden I see – a couple of paces away – a robin; he seems to want to say something, or at least to keep one company: tiny pedestrian, already marked out as cats' prey. How to convey the colour of his breast? Not so much pink, or purple, or blood red, as brick red; though the word prompts notions of wall, of stone itself, the sound of stone shattering, which one has to dismiss in favour of other associations: tamed fire, reflections of fire; a colour you would call friendly, a redness that has utterly lost all sense of blaze, cruelty, war or triumph. In its plumage, earthy as the ground on which it delights to walk, the bird carries this sort of scarf whose colour is tamed fire, sky at sunset. It's almost nothing, just as the bird is almost nothing, and this moment, these tasks, these words. Barely a flying spark, or a little flag-bearer, messenger without a real message: the unfathomable strangeness of colours. It would weigh almost nothing, even in the palm of a child.

Meanwhile there reaches the ear, now and then, the slight, almost wary sound of the fig tree's last leaves; and fuller, but more distant, that of tall plane trees in a park; it's the stirring of the invisible wind, the sound the invisible makes. And in its shelter we go about our duties, the robin and I. He, the lantern-holder, the risk-taker, when there's a cat on the prowl.

Jacques Réda

JACQUES RÉDA was born in 1929, in the town of Lunéville in the Lorraine. His grandfather manufactured bicycles, marked with the brand name, *Établissements Réda*. Jacques Réda was sent to school with the Jesuits at Evreux, where he studied Classics, poetic prosody and theatre, and in 1953 he moved to Paris, the city he has lived in (and written about) ever since. After some early publications, which he later judged "premature", there was a long period that produced little poetry, when he worked as a critic for *Jazz Magazine*, which he co-founded. He leapt to prominence with the publication of *Amen* (Gallimard, 1968), which won the Prix Max Jacob. This inaugural volume, and the two that followed it, *Récitatif* and *La Tourne*, marked the arrival of a major new voice, and one quite at odds with the nihilistic minimalism of the period, in that it reinstated a passionate and turbulent lyrical utterance. Equally striking and original were the densely-textured prose poems that make up *Les Ruines de Paris* (1977), which cast Réda as a true successor to the great poet-*flâneurs* of the past. The triumph of *Les Ruines* encouraged Réda to continue in this direction, and helped forge his unique mixture of peripatetic observation and (frequently humorous) metaphysical speculation, all done in a singularly companionable style. When in 1987 he became editor-in-chief of the *Nouvelle Revue Française* he naturally enough introduced new voices, or voices that had been marginalized and obscured, some of which belonged recognizably to his own poetic "constituency". His work at the *NRF* did not apparently inhibit his own production, and books of prose and collections of poetry flowed from his pen. The major volumes include *Hors les murs* (1982), *L'Herbe des talus* and *Le bitume est exquis* (1984), *Celle qui vient à pas légers* (a treatise on prosody, 1985), *Retour au calme* (1989), *Le Sens de la marche* (1990), *La Liberté des rues* (1997), *L'Adoption du système métrique* (2004), *Ponts flottants* (2006). Réda also publishes fellow poets in a sporadic series of small "brochures", hand-written and produced by himself, entitled *Le petit poëte illustré*.

Pluie du matin

Je rassemble contre mon souffle
Un paysage rond et creux qui me précède
Et se soulève au rythme de mon pas. La rue
Penche, brisée en travers des clôtures.
Le jour qu'on ne voit pas lentement se rapproche,
Poussé par les nuages bas,
Décombres fumants de l'espace.
Des cafés à feux sourds restent ancrés à la périphérie
Où roulent des convois, la mer
Sans fin dénombrant ses épaves.
Je tiens ce paysage contre moi,
Comme un panier de terre humide et sombre,
La pluie errante en moi parcourt
L'aire d'une connaissance désaffectée.

Morning Rain

Against each breath I gather
a rounded, dipping landscape that runs ahead
and swells to the rhythm of my pace. The road
inclines, cut across by fences.
Unseen day is slowly drawing closer,
driven on by low clouds,
the smoking debris of space.
Dimly-lit cafés rest at anchor on the rim
where trains roll by, the sea
forever counting up its wrecks.
This is the landscape I clasp to me
like a basket of dark, damp earth;
the rain roaming through me explores
familiar, deconsecrated space.

Prière d'un passant

Toi qui peux consoler, dieu des métamorphoses, vois
Le désordre uniforme de vivre et comme je suis las.
Je voudrais devenir une pierre et rêver ta gloire
Obscurément, comme rêvent l'ardoise et le charbon.
Ou bien fais-moi semblable à cette aile d'espace
Qui vibre à peine sur les toits et le long des façades
Quand le soir m'ouvre l'amitié muette des maisons.
Mais ne me laisse pas, entre la rue et les nuages,
Contre la marche bleue heurter mon crâne; casse-le,
Répands-le dans ta douceur d'ardoise et d'horizon.

Prayer of a Passer-By

Because you offer consolation, god of metamorphoses, see
the chaotic sameness of living and how I'm weary.
I wish I could become a stone and muse upon your glory
darkly, like the musing of slate or charcoal.
Or else shape me after that wing of space
that barely quivers on rooftops and along façades
as evening shows me the mute affability of houses.
But don't let me, between the road and the clouds,
hit my head against the blue step; smash it,
scatter it over your gentleness of slate and horizon.

Lettre à Marie

Vous m'écrivez qu'on vient de supprimer le petit train d'intérêt
    local qui, les jours de marché, passait couvert de poudre
    et les roues fleuries de luzerne.
Devant le portail des casernes et des couvents.
Nous n'avions jamais vu la mer. Mais de simples champs d'herbe
Couraient à hauteur de nos yeux ouverts dans les jonquilles.
Et nos effrois c'étaient les têtes de cire du musée,
Le parc profond, les clairons des soldats,
Ou bien ce cheval mort pareil à un buisson de roses.
Des processions de folle avoine nous guidaient
Vers les petites gares aux vitres maintenant crevées,
Abandonnées sans rails à l'indécision de l'espace
Et à la justice du temps qui relègue et oublie
Tant de bonheurs désaffectés sous la ronce et la rouille.
Depuis, nous avons vu la mer surgir à la fenêtre des rapides
Et d'autres voix nous ont nommés, perdus en des jardins.
Mais votre verger a gardé dans l'eau de sa fontaine
Le passé transparent d'où vous nous souriez toujours
Les bras chargés d'enfants et de cerises.
Je pense aux jours d'été où vous n'osez ouvrir un livre
À cause de ce désarroi de cloches sur les toits.
N'oubliez pas.
Dites comme nos mains furent fragiles dans la vôtre –
Et qu'ont-ils fait de la vieille locomotive ?

Letter to Marie

You write to say they've scrapped the little local train that
    on market days came by covered in dust, its wheels
    wreathed in lucern.
Past the gates of the barracks and the convents.
We had never seen the sea. But plain fields of grass
ran level with us wide-eyed among the daffodils.
And what frightened us were wax heads in the museum,
the deep park, the soldiers' bugles,
or that dead horse looking like a rose bush.
Processions of wild oats led us on
to little stations, their windows smashed,
tracks gone, abandoned to the vacillations of space
and the judgment of time that locks away and forgets
so many joys estranged amid brambles and rust.
Since then we've seen the sea rise in the windows of fast
    trains
and other voices have spoken our names, astray in gardens.
But your orchard has kept in its fountain pool
the transparent past where you smile at us still
your arms full of children and cherries.
I think of summer days when you dare not open a book
because of that tumult of bells on the rooftops.
Don't forget.
Say how fragile our hands were in yours –
and what have they done with the old locomotive?

Les Ruines de Paris

(EXTRAIT)

Déjà vers le fond traversé de présences heureuses qui s'attardent, passent, reviennent, gens du soleil, l'espace demeure méticuleusement creusé dans cette matière friable et mate: le jour de Paris en hiver. À l'angle de la rue de Vaugirard une petite boucherie, seul souvenir du faubourg ancien, et ça pourrait être autrement n'importe quel carrefour, n'importe quel immeuble, plus bas, celui-là que j'observe, avec au cinquième étage l'éternel balcon des adieux. Je ne serais pas étonné d'y voir une main réapparaître, mais cette fois pour m'appeler, et le temps redeviendrait alors une longue pente de sable, très pâle et très fin comme il en existe en forêt, lumineux encore dans la nuit qui veut qu'on se sépare, et qu'une main de nouveau s'éternise pour ce geste d'adieu. Je ne suis plus moi-même à présent qu'un souvenir qui divague, se perdant de rue en rue jusqu'à l'éblouissement des ponts, parmi ces passants que le soleil d'hiver imagine.

Les Ruines de Paris

(EXTRACT)

In its depths now, criss-crossed by blithe presences who linger, move on, come back – people of the sun – space is still the hollow meticulously scooped from this dulled, crumbling substance: a winter's day in Paris. On the corner of rue de Vaugirard, a small butcher's shop – sole reminder of the old suburb, otherwise it could be any cross-roads, and that could be any apartment block, the one I'm looking at, further down, the fifth-floor balcony forever with its good-byes. I wouldn't be surprised if a hand reappeared, but for once beckoning to me, and then time would revert to a falling sweep of the palest, finest sand, as in forests, still luminous in the night that will see us part company, a hand raised again and forever in that farewell. All I am now is a memory wandering lost from street to street as far as the dazzle of bridges, among these passers-by the winter sun dreams up.

Deux vues de Bercy

Il est évident que le soleil s'arrête et ne bougera plus.
Comme au fond de champs gris sous les tours se reposerait
    une faneuse,
sa face rose à travers les branches luit sur les toits de Bercy.
Je tourne entre le milieu du fleuve et le parvis blond de
    l'église,
je suis comme le démon variable de l'immobilité.
Là des sables adoucis marquent les étapes de la décrue,
paupières superposées vers le retour au sommeil de l'eau;
ici j'aperçois une timide servante de la lumière:
dans un recoin mauve de grange plein de mousse elle se
    penche de profil,
les mains au creux du tablier parce que *l'ouvrage est faite*,
et que dans le silence heureux de sa tête les derniers mots sont
    dits.
J'ai appelé un chat roux qui s'est assis par politesse,
qui n'attend qu'un délai convenable pour pouvoir repartir.
Je le sens compréhensif mais la circonstance l'embarrasse;
il s'enfonce dans son poil et cligne bien chanoinement des
    yeux.
Alors une pie s'envole et, du pont de la gare de la douane,
roule le grondement d'un train moelleux, entre le fer et le
    pavé,
comme le corps assoupi du temps quand il se retourne en rêve
(et rêvant qu'il s'entend dormir dans le silence de Paris,
où je fais grincer ce petit volet aux boîtes du bureau de poste).

Two Views of Bercy

I

The sun has plainly come to a standstill, and for good.
Like a hay-maker resting in grey fields with towers rising
    behind her,
a rosy face shines through branches onto the roofs of Bercy.
Circling between mid-river and the pale church forecourt,
I could be the changeable spirit of immobility.
Over there, smooth sands mark the river's staggered fall,
eyelids overlapping where the water dropped back to sleep;
here I see a retiring maidservant of the light:
in the purple nook of a moss-filled barn she leans in profile,
hands folded into her apron because *the work is done*,
and in her head's contented silence, last words have been
    spoken.
I've called to a ginger cat who politely comes and sits
and will be off again as soon as he decently can.
I feel he's sympathetic, but this isn't the time or place;
he hunkers into his fur and blinks in a most canonical way.
Now a magpie flies off, and from the custom-house railway
    bridge
comes the rumbling of a sleek train, between the metal and
    the paving,
like a body drowsy with time turning over in a dream
(and dreaming he can hear himself asleep in the silence of
    Paris,
where hinges squeak as I open the post office mailbox).

Depuis quand n'a-t-on pas utilisé l'étroit banc de pierre
ménagé dans un retrait de la balustrade, au pont de Tolbiac?
Les constructeurs avaient de ces principes ou prévenances,
    naguère,
pour les enfants, les amoureux, les flâneurs assez rares
qui se contentent d'apprécier les tas de sable en bas sur le quai
du fleuve immobile tout pailleté de reflets impressionnistes.
Une allée de gleditschias conduit jusqu'au pont du chemin de
    fer.
La surplombent d'un côté des donjons de style station
    thermale,
et de l'autre un avis de la lessive Saint-Marc QUI NETTOIE
    TOUT.
On voit aussi des bancs mais en fonte et bois sous les arbres
dont la base se fourre de touffes d'herbe, folle comme autour
    d'un puits.
Mais on ne rencontre jamais grand monde non plus dans ces
    parages;
même les clochards préfèrent des lieux d'une moindre
    austérité.
Seul le soir s'y prélasse, plongé dans une telle buée rose,
qu'elle rend en pâte de Sèvres les cubes qui broient la gare
    de Lyon
et que tous les platanes de Bercy croulent d'amour sur la rive.
Pourtant un peu de vent fait jouer, entre les piles du pont,
des mains dans des mailles de cheveux blonds qui flottent,
    comme à la proue
d'un chaland baptisé *Paulhan*, tout ce linge et le pavillon
noir à tête de mort blanche et deux os en X des pirates.

How long is it since anyone used the narrow stone bench
set in a recess of the balustrade on the Tolbiac bridge?
Builders then had principles and provided for
children, lovers, the rather occasional strollers
who are glad to survey the heap of sand on the quay below,
the unmoving river daubed with impressionist gleams.
A path lined with gleditschia trees leads to the railway
    bridge.
It's overlooked on one side by spa-style thick stone walls,
and on the other by a sign for Saint-Marc bleach that
    CLEANS EVERYTHING.
You also see benches, though of metal and wood, under
    trees
crammed with grass at the base like the riotous tufts round
    a well.
But you never meet anyone much in these parts either;
even the tramps prefer to go somewhere less austere.
Evening has the place to itself, settling deep in the kind of
    pink haze
that turns into Sèvres porcelain the blocks crushing the
    Gare de Lyon
and has all the plane trees of Bercy reeling with love by the
    river.
But a light gust plays between the piles of the bridge,
    running
fingers through the mesh of tawny tresses as they float by,
like that washing strung on the prow of the barge
    christened *Paulhan*
along with a pirate pennant, white skull-and-crossbones
    against the black.

Deux vues de Plaisance

I

Un ciel neutre épongeant ses moindres velléités d'averse,
on compterait sans peine les points de chute des gouttes sur le
    trottoir:
il a plu dans un périmètre de moins de trois pas sur quatre;
bien avant de toucher terre tout le reste s'est diffusé dans le
    gris.
C'est une espèce de compagnie et de menace plutôt douces,
invitant à prendre verre sur verre dans les nombreux cafés.
Où se croisent la rue Raymond-Losserand et la rue de
    Gergovie,
il y a *Le Soleil d'Or*, *Au Bouquet* et *Le Réveil* (aujourd'hui
fermé pour cause de réunion familiale), puis à l'angle
de la rue du Moulin-de-la-Vierge, énigmatiques, *Les Ex*
dont six poivrots patibulaires veulent préserver l'énigme.
Enfin au coin de la rue Decrès, face aux *Salons Lenoir*
exposant des photos de leurs espaces pour banquets et noces,
la Maison Barbazange à cent ans et cent lieues de Paris.
Les murs n'ont pour tout ornement qu'une carte de France
    jaunâtre,
et le patron abandonne à regret sa belote pour servir.
Dehors les couleurs innocentes s'éprouvent et se concentrent;
on sent quelle attention à soi vient combler le vert et le bleu –
surtout le vert de la mauvaise herbe, heureuse, exubérante,
sachant que rien ne pourra jamais rien contre elle qui vaincra
    tout.

Two Views of Plaisance

I

Now that a neutral sky has mopped up every last impulse
    to pour,
you'd have no problem counting where the drops have hit
    the pavement:
it has rained on an area less than three paces by four;
long before touching earth the rest all misted into the grey.
It's companionable and menacing, in a rather agreeable way,
encouraging glass after glass in the numerous cafés.
Where rue Raymond-Losserand meets rue de la Gergovie,
there's *Le Soleil d'Or*, *Au Bouquet* and *Le Réveil* (today
closed for a family reunion), then on the corner
of rue du Moulin-de-la-Vierge: the enigmatic *Les Ex*,
its enigma duly preserved by six hang-dog boozers.
Lastly, at the corner of rue Decrès – opposite *Salons Lenoir*
where photos display their halls for banquets and weddings –
Maison Barbazange, a hundred years and a hundred leagues
    from Paris.
By way of decoration the walls have only a yellowing map
    of France,
and the *patron* grudgingly quits his card game to take orders.
Outside, innocent colours put themselves to the test and
    concentrate;
you can sense the self-consciousness overwhelming the green
    and the blue –
especially the green of the cheery, exuberant weeds
who know nothing can ever assail them, all-round winners
    in the end.

II

Une expression de bonté dans le profil du bossu fait place,
quand il se retourne, au douloureux étonnement de Méphisto,
les sourcils fins arqués très haut ouvrant sur l'injustice
des yeux où vrille intermittente une pointe de méchanceté.
Mais revoici le nez bonasse et lourd sous le feutre, la bouche
        épaisse
qui souffle exactement comme se dégonfle un pneu de vélo,
projetant au niveau du comptoir des flocons de mousse de
        bière
et s'aplatissant sur elle-même avec satisfaction.
On voit du pain et du jambon dans son sac en plastique:
avant d'aller mâchonner seul il boit encore un demi,
tandis qu'exalté comme Néron et livide comme une folle
le patron donne sa collection de foulards à contempler.
J'en désigne un bleu ciel à pois cramoisis pour cette noce
où rien ne conviendra mieux, dit-il, qu'un costume beige
        ou gris.
Il ajoute: « c'est très sobre, et je me suis lassé des cravates,
et l'été, quand ma femme et moi nous irons au Maroc,
je pourrai porter la même avec un blazer bleu marine,
non? » – Si. Tout le monde approuve. On ne sait pas ce qu'en
        pense le bossu
qui s'éloigne de travers cherchant l'obscur métro Plaisance,
ou ce pan coupé d'immeuble où flambe la station Pernety.

II

The kindly expression the hunchback wears in profile
gives way, when he turns round, to Mephisto's stunned
    grief,
the fine brows steeply arched, opening onto the eyes'
injustice where every so often malice drills a point.
But now the good-humoured nose is back, weighty under
    the felt hat, the fleshy mouth
wheezing like a bike tyre when the air's let out,
sending flurries of beer foam across the counter
and flattening down on itself with satisfaction.
There's bread and ham showing through his plastic bag:
before he goes to chew on it by himself, he drinks another
    half,
while the *patron*, hot-headed as Nero and livid as a
    madwoman,
presents his collection of silk scarves for appraisal.
I pick out one that's sky-blue dotted with crimson for the
    wedding
where a suit in grey or beige, he says, would be best.
He adds: "It's very sober, and I've had enough of ties,
and in the summer when my wife and I go to Morocco
I could also wear it with a navy-blue jacket,
no?" – Why, yes. Everyone approves. There is no knowing
    what the hunchback thinks
as he slopes off looking for the darkened Plaisance métro,
or that slab of building where Pernety station blazes out.

Un voyage aux sources de la Seine

(EXTRAIT)

À proprement parler, la Seine commence après le deuxième bassin: un fin ruisselet sans profondeur qui chuchote à peine sur des cailloux, puis va se perdre dans un haut fouillis d'herbes et de fleurs vaporeuses. Pour comprendre qu'il s'agit de la Seine, il faut un acte de foi. Ensuite on se représente le cours entier du fleuve qui naît ici et, nonchalant, avec tout le réseau d'affluents qui l'augmentent et reçoivent eux-mêmes les leurs, glisse jusqu'à la mer depuis des horizons de temps inconcevables. Et c'est bien le même fleuve qui, simultanément, sort de terre, chemine et va se perdre dans la Manche, et nous appelons bien le même ce fleuve dont le flot se renouvelle sans arrêt. Je considérais avec émerveillement les premiers pas de cette eau enfantine, qui s'éloigne les pieds nus sans rien savoir du destin qui lui est tracé, mais qu'elle réinvente et réaccomplit identique à mesure, le long des berges de Valvins ou de Croisset, sous les ponts qui s'efforcent de la rythmer comme un poème qui serait à lui-même sa mémoire, dont le sens serait l'oubli. Je m'agenouillai pour y tremper les lèvres, avec circonspection. Un rayon doré passait lentement d'arbre en arbre au sommet de la pente, parmi les claquements d'éventail des merles et des ramiers.

Un voyage aux sources de la Seine

(EXTRACT)

The Seine properly speaking begins after the second pool:
a thin, shallow stream barely whispers over the stones
before it's lost in a tangle of tall grass and misty flowers. To
grasp that this is the Seine requires an act of faith. Then
you imagine the entire course of the river that is born here
and, swollen by a whole network of tributaries – as they are,
in turn, by theirs – has been nonchalantly gliding down to
the sea from horizons of inconceivable time. And it's a
single river that issues from the ground, makes its way and
disappears into the Channel, all at the same time, and we
have the same name for this river whose flow is constantly
being renewed. I gazed in wonder at the first steps of this
infant water, setting off barefoot with no idea of the destiny
already marked out for it, but which it reinvents and re-
enacts identically phase by phase along the banks of Valvins
or Croisset, under bridges that do their best to give it the
rhythm of a poem that might serve as its memory, whose
meaning is oblivion. I knelt there to wet my lips, watchfully.
A shaft of gold moved slowly from tree to tree on the crest
of the slope, amid the fan-clattering of blackbirds and
woodpigeons.

Pont des Arts

À gauche la ville n'est plus un dédale de pierre,
Mais un très léger monument de cendre ou de poussière
Qui s'effondre sans bruit sous le poids du brouillard
Puis reparaît un peu plus loin, toujours plus vague,
Comme un rêve dans le sommeil bousculé d'un malade,
Entre les longues mains tâtonnantes des ponts.
Et j'avance parmi d'autres formes qui se défont
Sur la neige des quais, vers les jardins interminables.

Pont des Arts

To my left, the city that was a maze of stone
is now an airy monument of ash or dust
sinking without a sound beneath the weight of mist
and reappearing further off, but fainter,
like something dreamt in a fever-tossed sleep,
between the long groping hands of bridges.
And on I go among other shapes unravelling
on snowy embankments, towards gardens with no end.

L'amour

À sept heures les femmes sont belles et fatiguées.
Elles sortent à flot des banques, des magasins.
Peu songent à l'amour encore, elles ne sont touchées
Que par le rayon qui descend sous les branches de juin.
Mais tout le poids de la douceur qui les habite
Passe dans leurs talons aigus et sèchement crépite
Comme une immense machine à écrire sur les pavés.
Et j'écoute au fond du jardin ce froissement d'étoffes
Qui se confond avec le vent brassant d'épaisses touffes
De fleurs contre l'œil sans paupière et sans larmes du soir,
Jusqu'à l'heure où l'amour les prend et puis les abandonne.
Le ciel sombre est alors pareil à leur regard
Qui tient longtemps sa profondeur ouverte pour personne.

Love

At seven o'clock the women are tired and lovely
drifting out on a tide from banks and shops.
Few as yet have thoughts of love, feeling only
the touch of a ray that slips below June branches.
But the weight of gentleness that dwells in them
shifts to their stiletto heels, the dry patter
of a mighty typewriter on the paving-stones.
And from the garden I listen to the rustle of fabrics
mingling with the wind as it stirs dense clusters
of blossom against the unblinking, tearless eye of dusk,
until love plucks them and then discards them.
That is when the darkened sky is like their gaze
lingering on to reveal its depths, for no one.

La bicyclette

Passant dans la rue un dimanche à six heures, soudain,
Au bout d'un corridor fermé de vitres en losange,
On voit un torrent de soleil qui roule entre des branches
Et se pulvérise à travers les feuilles d'un jardin,
Avec des éclats palpitants au milieu du pavage
Et des gouttes d'or en suspens aux rayons d'un vélo.
C'est un grand vélo noir, de proportions parfaites,
Qui touche à peine au mur. Il a la grâce d'une bête
En éveil dans sa fixité calme: c'est un oiseau.
La rue est vide. Le jardin continue en silence
De déverser à flots ce feu vert et doré qui danse
Pieds nus, à petits pas légers sur le froid du carreau.
Parfois un chien aboie ainsi qu'aux abords d'un village.
On pense à des murs écroulés, à des bois, des étangs.
La bicyclette vibre alors, on dirait qu'elle entend.
Et voudrait-on s'en emparer, puisque rien ne l'entrave,
On devine qu'avant d'avoir effleuré le guidon
Éblouissant, on la verrait s'enlever d'un seul bond
À travers le vitrage à demi noyé qui chancelle,
Et lancer dans le feu du soir les grappes d'étincelles
Qui font à présent de ses roues deux astres en fusion.

The Bicycle

Going down the street one Sunday at six, suddenly
At the end of a passageway framed with diamond panes,
You see a torrent of sun rolling through branches
And sending the finest spray onto garden leaves,
With patches of light quivering on the flagstones,
And gold suspended in droplets from the spokes of a bike.
It's a large black bicycle, perfectly proportioned,
Barely touching the wall. It has the grace of an animal
On the alert in its calm intentness: it is a bird.
The street is empty. Without a sound the garden keeps
Pouring these fiery streams of green and gold that dance
Barefoot, in small light steps on the chill of the stones.
Now and then a dog barks, as if at the edge of a village.
You think of walls lying tumbled, of woods and pools.
Then the bike begins to vibrate, as if it can hear.
And though you would like to seize it, unchained as it is,
You sense that even before you'd stroked the dazzling
Handlebars, you would see it take off in a single bound
Right through the half-drowned, wobbling panes of glass,
And fling on the evening's fire the clusters of sparks
That have turned its wheels into these conjoined stars.

Les pommes de Jules Renard

(EXTRAIT)

V. *Sort imprévu de la deuxième pomme*

C'est un très beau cheval d'un noir rouge, l'œil en velours ténébreux. Il vient dès que je l'appelle, au pas du fond de son pré pelé, et happe consciencieusement chaque bout de pain que je lui tends sur ma main ouverte. Quand je n'en ai plus, j'arrache une grosse touffe d'herbe, épanouie dans l'humidité de la haie. Il pense que c'est le légume et l'avale avec le même appétit. J'essaye de profiter de sa gourmandise pour lui témoigner de l'affection, lui gratter la crinière, lui flatter le col. Il encense, parce que ça l'agace, ou peut-être pour dire merci. De ce gros œil velouté si complètement impénétrable, je me demande s'il me voit vraiment. On dirait plutôt qu'il m'ignore, mais ce n'est pas cela non plus. Il me perçoit avec une rare précision, au contraire, mais ne m'intériorise pas. Rien de moi ne se transmue en substance chevaline, à part le pain offert, où se sont transmués des épis d'un champ peut-être tout proche. Mais le pain vite mangé et ma forme disparue, que reste-t-il? L'œil de ce cheval ressemble à l'œil du ciel bientôt nocturne. L'étoile de vie qui brille au fond, un peu sanglante et sans mémoire, m'exclut. Une dernière poignée d'herbe – et j'avais oublié ce croûton. Et puis il faut décidément qu'on se quitte, ou bien je manquerai mon train. Mais à peine au milieu de la route, je l'entends qui tape du sabot. Quoi encore? J'ai oublié le dessert, et cette insistance m'attendrit. Je retraverse. J'ai la solution. Il faut voir comme il mâche cette pomme. À présent il me regarde partir. Comme j'ai recoiffé mon casque, il doute que je sois bien le même que l'être à pomme et à pain et, seul dans le poudroiement du soir sur les collines, s'éloigne au petit trot de la route d'Auxerre, où peut survenir n'importe quoi.

The Apples of Jules Renard

(EXTRACT)

V. *Unexpected fate of the second apple*

It's a very handsome horse, reddish-black, his eye dark velvet. He comes as soon as I call, ambling over from the far side of his stripped meadow, and dutifully scoffs every piece of bread I offer on my open palm. When I have no more, I tear a thick tuft from the grass that thrives in the damp of the hedgerow. He thinks it's the vegetable portion and gobbles it with the same relish. I try to take advantage of his gourmandise to demonstrate affection, scratching his mane, stroking his neck. He tosses his head in irritation, or perhaps to say thank you. So utterly impenetrable, that great velvet eye, I wonder if he's really seeing me. Rather it's as if he is taking no notice, but that isn't it either. On the contrary, he perceives me with a rare accuracy, but he does not internalize me. Nothing of me is transmuted into equine matter, apart from the bread I gave, those transmuted ears of corn that might have come from a nearby field. But with the bread soon eaten and me gone, what is left? The eye of this horse is like that of the sky with night about to fall. The starry twinkle of life deep within, a bit bloodshot and with no memory, excludes me. A last fistful of grass – and that crust I had overlooked. And then we really have to part ways, or I'll miss my train. But I am barely halfway across the road when I hear him stamp his hoof. What is it now? I've forgotten the dessert, and such insistence wins me over. Back I cross. I have the solution. You should see him munch that apple. Now he is watching me leave. As I have put my helmet back on, he can't be sure I am the same being as the one with the bread and the apple, and all alone as evening dusts the hills, he trots off, away from the road to Auxerre, where anything might happen.

Reconnaissance

Ils se tenaient au bord du trottoir, comme en expectative, alors qu'un feu venait de m'arrêter et que l'espace des quais et du pont, jusqu'aux guichets du Louvre, débordait de mon rétroviseur. Parce que des gens qui ne font pas trop attention d'habitude, quand ils affrontent isolément des flots de circulation, témoignent d'une grande prudence s'ils traînent le dimanche en famille. Oui, un peu comme des animaux (mais c'est du temps qu'ils broutent), ils se regroupent aux points délicats – des espèces de gués ou de lisières – et, avec circonspection, flairent de tous côtés l'étendue amplifiée par le silence. Un petit troupeau: le père, la mère, trois ou quatre faons. Mais je n'observais que l'aîné qui tirait un peu en arrière, à l'état le plus délié d'un équilibre éphémère et souverain: entre nonchalance et promptitude, ingénuité et génie, tout songe, tout élan. Lui-même, alors (sinon comment me permettre cette insistance), n'avait d'yeux que pour mon vélomoteur. Un modèle très ordinaire. Mais cela il le notait aussi, procédant à son examen avec l'acuité d'une certaine compétence en mécanique (où je n'entends rien), sans pour autant se défendre d'une émotion toute distincte de la convoitise: un pur et simple émerveillement. Et je dirais presque une gratitude, comme si le seul spectacle de ce possible de vitesse et d'indépendance l'avait ravi. Au redémarrage (comme de juste ils s'étaient décidés un peu trop tard, en bousculade), nos regards se sont croisés, chacun prenant acte de la sagacité bienveillante de l'autre, d'un sourire l'approuvant – oh, une seconde, une infime goutte de temps devenue ce diamant qui paie une vie.

Acknowledgement

They were standing on the kerb, as if in expectation, just as
a traffic-light had halted me, and the expanse of embank-
ments and bridges overflowed my rearview mirror all the
way to the ticket offices of the Louvre. Because people who
don't usually pay much attention when facing streams of
traffic on their own, become very cautious when they're
whiling away a Sunday with the family. Yes, rather like
animals (though it is time they are grazing on), they re-
group in exposed places – fords or clearings of a sort – and
warily sniff all around as silence expands the open space. A
small herd: the father, the mother, three or four fawns. But
I was watching only the eldest who, lagging behind a little,
was given over entirely to a moment's supreme equilibrium:
between nonchalance and alertness, ingenuousness and
genius, all dream, all impulse. He, meanwhile (otherwise
how could I let myself dwell on the matter), couldn't take
his eyes off my moped. A very ordinary model. But he noted
that fact, too, pursuing his inspection with the shrewdness
of someone with a grasp of mechanics (which I cannot
fathom), while at the same time allowing himself to feel
something quite distinct from covetousness: a pure and
simple wonderment. Almost gratitude, I would say, as if
the mere sight of this intimation of untold speed and inde-
pendence had entranced him. Moving off again (they had
decided just too late, of course, to make a dash for it) our
eyes met, each of us noting the other's genial discernment
and approving smile – oh, a moment, an infinitesimal drop
of time become this diamond worth a lifetime.

L'écluse

Alors que le train suivait depuis longtemps le cours de ma
    tristesse
(non: c'était presque une épouvante – mais hurler dans ce
    compartiment?)
la vision d'un canal avec une écluse en manœuvre
m'apaisa.
Ensuite j'aperçus deux péniches et d'autres signes de vie
au fond de l'opulence accablante où la plaine s'étalait.
Ainsi devant ces vantaux tournant et cette cascade,
l'étendue – un instant avant encore dévastée – a repris sens
et, bien qu'il eût aussitôt plongé dans un virage,
par ce bouillonnement d'eau trouble en moi j'ai changé de
    bief.

The Lock

For a long while the train had followed the course of my
    sadness
(no: it was more like terror – but to shriek in this
    compartment?)
when the sight of lock gates being manoeuvred on a canal
calmed me.
Next, two barges and other signs of life caught my eye
amidst the oppressive lushness of the outspread plain.
So that set against those turning sluice-gates and that
    cascade,
the expanse – a moment earlier still stricken – made sense
    once more
and, though the water had then plunged into a curve,
thanks to its troubled churning in me, I switched levels.

Le vertige

Ah le vertige de l'horizontale dans une plaine sans fin,
une de ces plaines bien plates où l'on franchit des rideaux
    d'arbres,
des averses, des prés, des bois sans épaisseur
et où repassent les boucles d'une rivière peut-être toujours
    la même
(on ne sait pas).
C'est un vertige dont l'attirance n'est pas celle de la chute
mais d'une régulière et continuelle progression.
L'infini court au fil de l'herbe,
                              on n'arrivera jamais au but.
Eh bien il n'y en a pas et ce n'est pas non plus ce qu'on
    désire
mais avancer ainsi dans la platitude extatique
sous le ciel bombé où s'appuient des échelles de nuages
    sans barreaux.
Nord, est, ouest, sud, peu importe, il n'y a plus de points
    cardinaux.
Rien que le magnétisme diffus mais puissant de l'étendue
    aspirant dans la bonne direction,
la seule,
pour entrer plus profond à chaque pas dans l'intimité
    muette de tout.

Vertigo

Ah, the dizzy horizontal of a plain without end,
one of those really flat plains where you pass through
    curtains of trees,
rain-showers, meadows, woods with no depth,
where meandering loops could be all the same river
(you can't tell).
It's a vertigo enticing not with a sheer drop
but steady unbroken progress.
Infinity runs through a blade of grass,
              you'll never reach where you're aiming for.
Well anyway there's no such thing and nor do you want it
but only to move along in ecstatic flatness
beneath a curved sky propping stepless ladders of cloud.
North, east, west, south, no matter, the cardinal points
    have gone.
Nothing but the strong magnetic sweep of wide space
    aiming for the right direction,
the only way
to enter more deeply, with every step, the mute affinities
    everywhere.

Tashi à quatre ans

Un peu de moi part en trottant
   En maillot de bain rouge.
À peine si l'océan bouge.
   Un peu d'elle pourtant
Fuit déjà sans qu'on le soupçonne,
   Puisque – moi disparu –
Jamais elle n'aura couru
   Aussi bien pour personne
Jusqu'aux étincelles du pli
   Que la mer renouvelle
En montant vers le seau, la pelle,
   Jalons de l'oubli.

Tashi Aged Four

A little of me goes trotting off
   In a bright red swimsuit.
The ocean's barely stirring.
   But a little of her is already
Slipping away without our knowing,
   Since – with me gone –
She will never have run
   So well for anyone else
Out to the sparkling pleat
   The sea folds over anew
Rising towards the spade and bucket
     That mark out our forgetting.

Paul de Roux

PAUL DE ROUX was born in 1937 into an artistic family in the Provençal town of Nîmes. He moved to Paris where, at the age of twenty, he was taken on by the publishing firm of Robert Laffont, where he worked for the next thirty or so years. While his career offers little to record in terms of outward incident, the very fact of being desk-bound in an office for so long leaves a deep groove in his writing, the lassitude and the frustration acting at times like the grain of sand in an oyster shell. The titles of his successive collections published by Gallimard are reveal-ing in this respect – *Entrevoir* (1980), *Le Front contre la vitre* (1987), *Poèmes de l'aube* (1990), *La Halte obscure* (1993), *Le Soleil dans l'œil* (1998) and *À la dérobée* (2005): the poems record stolen instants of vision, even occasionally of euphoria – but equally of discouragement and despair. Paul de Roux was undoubtedly one of the new lyrical voices fostered by Jacques Réda at the *NRF*. During his latter years with Laffont, he worked almost exclusively on overhauling the celebrated Laffont *Dictionnaire* of French literature – the *Dictionnaire des œuvres* and the *Dictionnaire des auteurs* – the whole work, in several volumes, being vastly expanded under de Roux's editor-ship. For several years during the 1970s and 1980s de Roux also edited, in his own time, a handsomely produced little magazine, *La Traverse*. Like others in this group, Paul de Roux has pub-lished a considerable body of writing culled from his ongoing notebooks, or *carnets*; there are now four sizeable volumes of these. (They are published by Le temps qu'il fait, an important publisher of contemporary poetry based in Cognac). De Roux has published a translation of Keats, and a long *Poème des saisons* (1989). He has also written some engaging prose meditations, frequently based on his experience of looking at paintings, notably the *Visites à Simon Vouet* (1999), and a narrative based on the life of Rembrandt, *Une double absence* (2000).

La rue profonde

Un grand pan de brume, si grand
qu'il t'enveloppe complètement, toi
et la ville et l'origine des hommes:
manteau gluant d'humidité ou, mieux,
tombeau où sans cesse tu roules, quand bien même
on te verrait chaque jour rentrer par la même rue,
rue qui est pour toi une sentine fétide
quand le soleil du plein été resplendit
sur les arbres et les âmes des hommes
qui ont porté la dalle de leur tombeau
comme le paralytique son grabat et soulevé
du même coup les nuages pour faire passer
alentour la lumière dans la rue profonde.

The Deep Street

A broad patch of mist, so broad
it envelops you completely, you
and the city and the origin of men:
a coat clammy with damp, or rather
a tomb you turn in endlessly, even though
you're seen taking the same street home each day,
a street that for you is a fetid alley
when the high summer sun is shining
on the trees and on the souls of men
who have taken up their tombstone
as the cripple took up his bed, so lifting
the clouds to send light flowing
round and into the deep street.

La pluie

Si tu pouvais t'enrouler dans ce voile de pluie,
gouttes sur les paupières et au creux de la main,
peut-être pourrais-tu te reposer: la déchirure
c'est d'être là et de voir la pluie
qui ruisselle sur les carreaux, qui cingle
les arbres et leurs bourgeons, savoir
entrer dans une goutte de pluie est un secret
que bien peu connaissent sans doute:
c'est celui qui délie les membres
et rentre la création dans la mer
comme au premier jour, quand tout
n'était qu'en puissance dans l'écume.

The Rain

If you could wrap yourself in this veil of rain,
drops on the eyelids, on the upturned hand,
you might find some rest: the wrench
is being here and watching the rain
stream down the tiles, lash
the trees and their buds, while knowing
how to enter a raindrop is a secret
shared by very few, no doubt:
it is what unbinds the limbs
and takes creation back to the sea
as on the first day, when everything
was potential in the spume.

Encore le froid

Peupliers agités par le vent froid
dans la lumière basse, arasée,
la terre recluse en elle-même,
quelques feuilles encore sur le bouleau,
lampions éteints, un train passe au loin
évoquant le froid de la limaille,
la gare aux courants d'air glacial
où l'on a accompagné un ami, où les quais vides
sont la piste crissante vers les étoiles cachées.

The Cold Again

Poplars shaken by the cold wind
in a low, curtailed light,
the earth secluded within itself,
a few leaves still on the birch,
switched-off fairy-lights, a distant train
conveying the coldness of iron,
the station with its icy winds
where you saw off a friend, the empty platforms
a rasping trail towards the hidden stars.

Impromptu

Ici où tu voudrais conjurer le sort
qui t'enferme dans le hall d'une banque
attendant l'ouverture, piétinant,
tu te demandes ce qui peut être beauté,
consolation, tendresse entre ces vitres,
avec la vue sur l'avenue, les passants
de 8 h 50, pressés, les voitures
et pas un rayon de soleil, et tu vois
resplendir le langage, plante exquise.

Impromptu

It is here – wishing you could ward off fate
that has you cornered in the entrance to a bank
pacing up and down till it opens
– that you wonder about beauty,
consolation, tenderness inside these windows,
looking out on the avenue, people
hurrying past at 8.50 am, traffic
and not one ray of sun, and you see
shining the lovely plant of language.

Une jeune fille

Nue, la beauté est peut-être invisible,
c'est ce que je me dis en regardant ce visage
pur de tout maquillage, offert
aux voyageurs du métro, où la femme
est encore une jeune fille et le teint
non pas éclatant mais simplement juvénile
– et les traits désarment la description
que rien de singulier ne dépare
et que le terme «réguliers» trahirait:
c'est un visage perdu
en toi qui n'as pour l'accueillir
ni le creuset ni l'or où se gravent
les traits fugitifs, la grâce incertaine
de celle qui ne sait pas qu'un instant
elle est le mystère tout entier.

A Girl

Naked, perhaps beauty is invisible,
so I tell myself as I watch this face
innocent of all make-up, offered
to travellers on the métro, where the woman
is still a girl, her complexion
not radiant, simply youthful
– and her features defy description
having nothing unusual to mar them,
though "regular" would be a travesty:
it is a face lost
in you who have nothing to welcome it,
neither the crucible nor the gold engraved
with the fleeting lines, the hesitant grace
of one who does not know she is
that moment, the full extent of mystery.

Les étourneaux

Le dernier jour de l'année, en contrebas de la foule,
du bruit, au bord du fleuve obscur,
sur le quai au pavé raboteux, tu découvres
la double poignée de grains noirs jetée à travers ciel,
les deux bandes d'étourneaux, vol rapide,
vifs battements d'ailes, deux groupes comme jouant,
s'écartant, se confondant, se scindant
sous un ciel froid et venteux où tanguent
de si sombres nuages, tout à la fin du jour,
eux, les étourneaux, comme un signe de vie
englobant la vieille cathédrale, le dédale des rues,
comme si la terre avait besoin de leur témoignage,
comme si elle s'entendait dans leurs cris et pouvait
par eux respirer encore, et dans ta poitrine aussi
l'apaisement se fait avec le soir.

The Starlings

Last day of the year, down the hill from the crowd
and the noise, beside a dark river
on the rough-paved quay, you come upon
a double fistful of black grains thrown across the sky,
two flocks of starlings, fast-flying,
brisk wing-beats, the two groups as if at play,
separating, converging, splitting apart
under a cold windy sky where clouds
pitch so darkly, right at the day's end,
these starlings, like a sign of life
encircling the old cathedral, the maze of streets,
as if the earth needed their testimony,
as if it heard itself in their cries and could,
through them, keep breathing, and you too find
your heart soothed with the evening.

À la mémoire du peuplier noir

La leçon des grands arbres est cette croissance,
ce grand dessin contre le ciel pour nos yeux.
Un jour c'est la chute inéluctable,
l'air béant où s'élevait le fût,
les demeures de feuilles (quand la silhouette
d'un jet sur l'horizon le signait de son paraphe).
Rien, plus rien, retour au sans forme:
sciure dont s'est nourrie la terre ou fumée dans le ciel.
Le terme, amer, est celui-là
qui couronne peut-être le généreux élan
sans calcul vers la lumière, la course
qui a déployé cette forme éminente
vers les nuages, le soleil ou la pluie
et qui semblait nous abriter aussi, passants
(destructeurs de notre amour).
S'il est ainsi, celui-là, à l'entrée du parc,
effacé du sol et du ciel natifs,
qui es-tu, toi – cela t'effleure, tu l'oublieras –
pour refuser de t'éployer selon ton faible élan,
de retomber enfin, à l'image d'un arbre,
asile des oiseaux, des abeilles et des songes?

In Memory of the Black Poplar

The lesson from tall trees is this growing,
this grand design against the sky, for our eyes.
One day it's the inevitable fall,
the air gaping where the trunk once rose,
the abodes of leaves (when a jet outlined
on the horizon would sign it with a flourish).
Nothing, nothing left, back to formlessness:
sawdust to nourish the earth, or smoke in the sky.
The ending, bitter, is maybe
what crowns the generous
uncalculated leap towards the light, the spurt
that launches this outstanding form
towards the clouds, the sun or the rain
and seemed to shelter us too as we passed
(we who destroy our love).
If that's how it is, you there at the park gate,
blotted from native earth and sky,
who are you – lightly touched by this, bound to forget –
to refuse to stretch to your own paltry leap,
and fall again to earth in the end, like a tree,
refuge of birds, and bees, and dreams?

Il y a un mois encore

Imagine, imagine l'île déserte
et le navire maintenant disparu
et jamais, tu le sais, nul ne relâche ici.
Tu mourras seul dans ce lieu que tu n'as pas choisi
et cela, au cœur de la ville,
entouré de toute l'agitation des rues
tu aurais dû le savoir et que la main
que tu étendais vers sa chevelure
bientôt ne rencontrerait plus
qu'une peau de chèvre rêche
mal tannée et puante.

Only a Month Ago

Imagine, imagine the desert island
and the ship now gone
and nobody, you know it, ever calls in here.
You will die alone in this place you never chose
in the heart of the city, surrounded
by all the tumult of the streets
as you should have known, and that your hand
reaching out towards her hair
would soon encounter nothing
but a coarse, uncured
and stinking goatskin.

Un regard

Douce lumière des lointains
éclairant un clocher dans la plaine.
«La vitesse réduit l'espace»
dit le vieil homme. C'est fâcheux,
terre réduite à un grain de café
un jour nous échappe des mains
– souviens-toi, en ces jours-là
il y avait des chevaux aux abords des villages
et leur regard satisfait
quand, brouté un carré d'herbe,
ils levaient soudain la tête.
Dans le regard d'un alezan
la terre nous disait adieu.

A Gaze

Gentle light in the distant spaces
brightening a belltower on the plain.
"Speed reduces space"
says the old man. It's vexing,
earth reduced to a coffee bean
dropping from our hands one day
– do you remember there used to be
horses on the outskirts of villages
with that satisfied look
when, after cropping their fill of grass,
they suddenly raised their heads.
In the gaze of a chestnut mare
the earth bade us farewell.

Rue Beautreillis

Avec le temps ce visage
qui fut souriant peut-être
semble en pleurs, inexplicablement.
Le bas-relief se délite, s'obscurcit
et la figure au-dessus de la porte
est maintenant absente de la rue, toute
retournée à sa vie intime de pierre
et peu importe alors, passant,
ce qu'elle te semble.

Rue Beautreillis

With time this face
once smiling perhaps
seems inexplicably in tears.
The bas-relief crumbles and darkens
and the figure above the door
is now gone from the street, wholly
returned to its inward life of stone,
so it hardly matters, passer-by,
what it seems to you.

Les foins

Tard dans sa vie il se souvient
d'avoir enfant dévalé une meule de foin
crissante, chaude et dorée
– en septembre peut-être?
Les filles du fermier participaient au jeu,
première rencontre avec la féminité
qui l'émut: «Quel âge pouvais-je avoir?»
se demande-t-il aujourd'hui,
jour anniversaire, qu'il partage peut-être
avec une dame de soixante-cinq ans
qui se souvient au même instant
du foin, de ses sœurs, du petit garçon
inconnu, dont le visage est oublié:
reste l'exaltation d'un moment,
la glissade, jupe retroussée.

Haystack

Late in life he remembers
how as a child he slid down the hay,
the rasp of it, warm and golden
– was it September?
The farmer's daughters joined in the game,
a first encounter with femininity
and it moved him: "How old could I have been?"
he asks himself today,
his birthday, which perhaps he shares
with a lady aged sixty-five
who also this minute is thinking back
to the hay, her sisters, the little boy
they didn't know, his face now forgotten:
what stays is the thrill of that moment,
the swoop, the skirt flying up.

À la table du fond

La si discrète dame, tout au fond
de la brasserie, dans l'ombre,
arrivant chaque jour pour déjeuner, seule,
et se mettant à l'écart, là-bas,
dois-je saluer son indépendance?
déplorer sa solitude?
Je ne sais, je ne vois
qu'un infime reflet lumineux
dans les verres de ses lunettes.

At the Far Table

So discreet, the lady at the far end
of the café, in shadow,
who comes every day to lunch, alone,
who sets herself apart, over there,
should I hail her independence?
lament her loneliness?
I cannot tell, cannot see
anything but a tiny gleam of light
in the glass of her spectacles.

La bâche

Sur le grand échafaudage
un pan de bâche frémit, se soulève,
emblème de la vie des choses
que nous croyons mortes. Certes
plus assurées paraissent les pierres
du vieux mur, encore visibles:
proches des gargouilles, d'un temps
où la main de l'homme éprouvait
dans leur grain et leur rugosité
pierre, bois, avec la terre,
qui était «basse», on le sait,
mais parlait aussi, sans un mot,
d'un monde au-delà des hommes
et proche à toucher de la main,
telles les étoiles certains soirs.

The Tarpaulin

On the high scaffolding
a corner of tarpaulin shakes and bucks,
emblem of the life of things
we believe dead. The stones
of the old wall, still in view,
seem rather more secure:
closer to the gargoyles, to a time
when the hand of man felt
the roughness and the grain
of stone and wood, and the earth,
"lowly" though we know it was,
also spoke, wordlessly,
of a world beyond men
close enough for a hand to touch,
like the stars on certain evenings.

Till Eulenspiegel

De la petite radio, à côté du lit,
un filet de musique (crainte des voisins)
me parvient et, à cet instant,
j'aime Richard Strauss, j'aime la musique,
échappée nocturne hors de ma chambre
quand chaque note est un envol
au-delà de toute ville et de toute campagne
dans un monde uniquement sonore
et concret comme l'arête de la montagne.

Till Eulenspiegel

From the little radio beside the bed
a trickle of music (for fear of the neighbours)
reaches me, and suddenly
I love Richard Strauss, I love music,
night-time escapee from my room,
when each note takes off
beyond every city and every province
into a world uniquely of sound
and solid as a mountain ridge.

De jour en jour

Le temps qu'il fait, jusque sur les lames
du parquet a son reflet, éteint ou lumineux.
De jour en jour, on pourrait passer sa vie
à tenter d'apercevoir les variations printanières,
estivales, automnales, hivernales.
Et à l'instant fatal une lueur imprévue
nous surprendrait peut-être.

Day by Day

The weather has its own light
luminous or dull, even on the floorboards.
Day by day you could spend your life
trying to ascertain variations of spring,
summer, autumn, winter.
And at the fateful moment an unexpected
gleam might surprise us.

Au jour le jour

(EXTRAITS)

Le vent et le soleil, comme une immense partition qui vous maintiendrait à flot.

. . .

Est-ce le même scorpion que j'ai épargné il y a huit jours, le trouvant sous une pierre, et que je viens d'écraser bien malgré moi, marchant dans le noir? (Souviens-toi que le jardin est arène aussi.)

Après la mort d'un scorpion les étoiles semblent plus froides.

Nous ne savons absolument rien. Si au moins nous pouvions ne pas feindre. Si nous le pouvions ce serait sans doute comme de casser un carreau. Qu'est-ce qui viendrait: de l'air ou la mort?

. . .

Je regarde le jour aux fenêtres. C'est l'activité à laquelle je me serai livré avec le plus de constance.

. . .

Premier jour de l'automne. Hier, ce matin (7h) une chaleur tout à fait exceptionnelle pour la saison. Nostalgie de campagne avivée. Comme si ici tous les dons du ciel nous échappaient, panier percé. (Évidemment, je n'exclus pas que ce soit moi le panier percé.)

. . .

Le vent dégage. De même que les feuilles volent, quelque chose en nous bascule. L'allégresse communicative de la lumière est à l'œuvre. De petites ailes poussent aux pieds de plomb. L'instant est trop limpide pour ne pas faire oublier les heures, les années. Un instant.

Au jour le jour

(EXTRACTS)

Wind and sun, like an immense musical score that keeps you afloat.

. . .

Is it the same scorpion, the one I spared eight days ago when I found it under a stone, and that I just now crushed, quite accidentally, walking in the dark? (Remember that the garden is an arena too.)

After the death of a scorpion the stars seem colder.

We know absolutely nothing. If only we could stop pretending. If we could, it would probably be like breaking a window. What would come in: air or death?

. . .

I observe the day through the windows. This will turn out to be the most constant of my activities.

. . .

First day of autumn. Yesterday, and this morning (7 o'clock) exceptionally hot for the season. Yearning for the countryside revived. As if here, all heaven's plenty slips through a sieve. (Of course, I do not rule out the possibility that I am in fact the sieve.)

. . .

The wind blows clear. As the leaves fly, so something within us is shaken. The blitheness of the light is catching. Little wings sprout from feet of lead. The instant is too limpid not to efface the hours, the years. For an instant.

. . .

Le jour si beau derrière la vitre me laisse en plan, douloureux, impuissant, humilié. On voudrait que les mots se pressent contre les lèvres comme la lourde grappe. En fait on voudrait porter vraiment la grappe à ses lèvres. Sinon les mots eux-mêmes se fripent.

. . .

Je suis celui qui bute sur l'immédiat, qui est sans cesse ramené au petit cercle environnant. Je suis comme le chat Vladimir, que je vois assis derrière la vitre.

. . .

Selon que tu te laisses porter à l'exaspération ou à l'émerveillement, des poids considérables basculent. Certes, ce qui exaspère est actif, bruyant; c'est ce qui palabre aux radios, aux télés, ce qui fait claquer la langue de bois des journaux. Quand ce qui peut susciter l'émerveillement est muet (ou alors parole de merle), voilé, incertain, fugitif.

. . .

Mots, briques lourdes, froides, que tu prends une à une, que tu poses l'une sur l'autre. Même pas la promesse d'un mur. Ne serait-ce qu'un muret dressé contre toute les forces de dissolution que tu as trouvées à ton lever et qui t'ont accompagné à cette table. La métamorphose des briques ne t'appartient pas. Si elle ne se produit pas, tu peux élever le mur le plus haut: s'écroulant il ne fera que t'ensevelir sous son poids. Dans la métamorphose, le mur s'envole, chaque brique a soudain des ailes. (De toute façon, il n'en reste rien, il faut recommencer, sans plus d'assurance, une brique lourde et froide sur l'autre.)

. . .

. . .

The day behind my window so beautiful that I am left at a loss, aching, impotent, humiliated. One would like words to come pressing to one's lips like a heavy bunch of grapes. In fact, you'd really like to lift the bunch to your lips. Otherwise the words themselves get crushed.

. . .

I am someone who stumbles against the immediate, who is always brought back to the little circle around him. I am like Vladimir the cat, sitting there behind the glass.

. . .

According to whether you are given to exasperation or wonder, the balance can tip heavily either way. It's the active, noisy things that exasperate, that's certain; it's what babbles from the radio, the TV, what sets off the prattling cant of the newspapers. Whereas what arouses our wonder is silent (or else what the blackbird says), veiled, uncertain, fleeting.

. . .

Words, cold and heavy bricks that you choose one by one, and pile one on top of the other. Without even the certain prospect of a wall. Were it only a small brick wall raised against all the forces of dissolution you found when you got up, and that have come with you to this table. The bricks' metamorphosis does not depend on you. If it does not happen, then however high you build the wall, when it collapses it will only bury you under its weight. In meta-morphosis, the wall takes flight, each brick suddenly winged. (In any case, nothing remains of it, you have to begin again, with no greater certainty, one cold and heavy brick upon another.)

. . .

Cette étonnante formule d'Henri Raynal: «La parole emprunte les hommes. »

. . .

Pourquoi, songeant à la peinture d'Anne-Marie Jaccottet, le mot «comestible» m'est-il venu à l'esprit? Je crois qu'il évoquait pour moi les qualités sensibles des fruits, des fleurs, qui apparaissent immédiatement dans ces aquarelles, ces huiles. Ce sont des fruits (des paysages aussi bien) qui révèlent leur épiderme, si je puis dire. Un choix de couleurs, une façon de les poser qui évoquent la pulpe d'une pêche – et jusqu'au bourdonnement d'abeilles que l'on doit entendre au détour de cette allée. C'est un univers très coloré. Des aquarelles dans lesquelles les couleurs suffisent à donner ce caractère de «comestibilité» des choses. Non pas du tout l'envie de mordre dans ces fruits, non, on les voit plutôt comme on découvrirait des offrandes végétales aux pieds de divinités bouddhiques. Une sorte d'exaltation du visible dans le geste pur de l'offrande.

. . .

Seule une pensée d'au-delà de la terre peut nous rendre à nous-mêmes et à la terre.

. . .

Les vrais épistoliers vous donnent la note juste. Vous êtes étonné de ce qui vous échappe dans les réponses que vous leur faites. (En pensant à Henri Thomas).

An astonishing phrase from Henri Raynal: "Language borrows man."

. . .

Why, thinking of paintings by Anne-Marie Jaccottet, did the word "edible" come to mind? I think it expressed for me the tangible qualities of the fruits and flowers that figure strikingly in her oils and watercolours. These are fruits (and also landscapes) that reveal their skins, so to speak. A choice of colours and a way of applying them, that evoke the flesh of a peach – and even the buzzing of bees that can surely be heard where that path turns. It's a very colourful universe. Watercolours where the hues are enough to lend this "edible" quality to things. I don't mean the desire to bite into these fruits, not that at all, but rather that you see them the way you would discover harvest offerings at the foot of Buddhist gods. A sort of exaltation of the visible in the pure act of offering.

. . .

Only a thought from beyond the earth can return us to ourselves and to the earth.

. . .

Real masters of the epistolary art give you the right note. You are astonished at what comes out of you when you reply. (Thinking of Henri Thomas.)

Guy Goffette

GUY GOFFETTE was born in 1947 in the southernmost part of Belgium, an area bordering France known as the "Lorraine belge". This strangely "lost" part of the country, deeply provincial, provides the powerful imagery found in the collection that saw his coming of age as a poet, *Éloge pour une cuisine de province* (1988). Modest circumstances, a constrained childhood with its sporadic wild escapades, a deep melancholy – all these things are memorably voiced in the early poems. Goffette remained for many years in this part of Belgium, founding a family, and earning his living as a schoolteacher, a part-time bookseller and a publisher. Throughout the 1980s he edited and published a little magazine, *Triangle*. He also printed small poetry books, using letter-press, publishing under the name *L'Apprentypographe*. In his prose text "Partance" (2000) he takes refuge from the disturbances of family life in a ramshackle caravan at the end of the garden. Finally, Goffette quit his home in Belgium, and a new chapter of his life began, during which he travelled widely. From *La Vie promise* in 1991 his poetry was published by Gallimard. In addition to further collections of poetry – *Le Pêcheur d'eau* (1994), *Un manteau de fortune* (2001), *L'Adieu aux lisières* (2007) – Goffette has published three volumes in the Gallimard series *L'un et l'autre*: a text on one of his favourite poets, *Verlaine d'ardoise et de pluie* (1995); a meditation on the work of Bonnard and the role played by his wife Marthe, *Elle, par bonheur et toujours nue* (1998); and a biographical treatment of W. H. Auden, *L'Œil de la baleine*. A poet of eclectic literary taste, as his poems on writers reveal, Goffette has done much to introduce the work of Auden to the French-speaking public, and he has also written on Philip Larkin. Now based in Paris, Goffette works as a reader and an editor for Gallimard.

Crépuscule, 2

La maison à veilleuse rouge dans l'impasse
tu attendais de grandir, le cœur
et les doigts tachés d'encre
pour y chercher des roses
À présent qu'une route à quatre bandes
la traverse tu es entré toi aussi sans savoir
dans la file qui fait reculer l'horizon
où cet enfant t'appelle qui n'a pas pu grandir
portant jour après jour en ses mains sombres
le bouquet rouge au fond du ciel
que tu n'as pas cueilli

At Dusk, 2

The house with the red lamp in the blind alley
and you waiting to grow up, heart
and fingers stained with ink
from searching the place for roses
Now that a four-lane highway crosses it
you too, unawares, have taken your place
in the line that distances the horizon
where the child that couldn't grow calls to you
day after day his dark hands bringing
to the sky's rim the red bouquet
you never picked

Crépuscule, 3

Les yeux jaunes des voitures le soir
tu les voyais déjà, enfant
détourer le pied des immeubles
et tu faisais pareil à table
avec la mer et les ciseaux dorés
ajustant patiemment sous la lampe
l'image à sa légende obscure.
À présent tu sais lire et tiens ferme
la barre de ta fenêtre sur le monde
où les immeubles s'écroulent
l'un après l'autre dans l'incendie
découvrant peu à peu la ligne
sous laquelle il te faudra descendre
descendre encore, paupières closes,
pour joindre les bords extrêmes de ta vie.

At Dusk, 3

In the evening watching the yellow-eyed cars
you – still a child – would see them
highlight the bases of buildings
and at the table you'd do the same
with the sea and gold-coloured scissors
working patiently under the lamp to fit
the picture to its shadowy legend.
Now that you know how to read you grip
the bar of your window on the world
where buildings go toppling
one upon the other in the blaze
to reveal little by little the line
under which you will have to go
and go lower still, eyelids closed
to join the furthest edges of your life.

Crépuscule, 4

Ce peu de mots ajustés aux choses de toujours
ce questionnement sans fin des gosses dans la journée
ces silences plus longs maintenant, à l'approche du soir
comme le soleil traversant la chambre vide
sur des patins, tout cela qui se perd
entre les lames du parquet, les pas, les rides
a fini par tisser la toile inaccessible
qui drape chacun des gestes du vieux couple
lui donne cet air absent des statues
prenant le frais dans la cour du musée
— et nul ne voit leurs ombres se confondre
enjamber le haut mur du temps
mais seulement l'échelle aux pieds de la nuit
l'échelle sans barreaux ni montants
d'une vie petite arrivée à son terme.

At Dusk, 4

These few words fitting things that never change,
these endless questions kids ask during the day,
these silences growing longer now, as evening comes
the way the sun glides over the empty room
like a skater, all of this – disappearing
between the floorboards, the footsteps, the wrinkles –
has finally woven a cloth of remoteness
that drapes every gesture the old couple makes
and gives them the absent look of statues
taking the air on the museum terrace
– and no one sees their mingled shadows
clambering over time's high wall
but only the ladder at the foot of night
the ladder with no rungs and no one climbing
from a little life that has run its course.

L'extrême été

Le voisin est mort mais l'échelle
est restée contre l'arbre qui s'enfonce
avec le soleil dans la chair ferme
des pommes et la gorge des petits maraudeurs.
Eux font feu de tout bois
et de la mort se fichent
comme des pommes qu'ils écrasent
l'une après l'autre, sans remords
gravissant le dernier échelon de la joie.

Deep into Summer

The neighbour is dead but the ladder
still leans against the tree that with the sun
sinks deep into the firm flesh
of apples and the young raiders' throats.
Nothing is out of bounds
and they couldn't care less about death
or the apples they're crushing
one by one, with no regrets
as they climb to joy's last rung.

Les enfants qui glissent dans nos paroles
comme des points-virgules, savent tout
et se souviennent de notre mal
à dire la vie qui passe et comme l'amour
est difficile. Ils glissent en chantant un doigt léger
dans l'échancrure du monde qui nous couvre
puis s'arrêtent la joue contre l'oreille du chat
avec un visage grave et si vite fermé
qu'il nous déséquilibre, nous jette hors du temps,
soudain muets comme près d'un puits plein de morts
alors que s'arrondit, margelle de nos jours,
de nos vaines paroles, la pupille du chat.

The children who slip in between our words
like semicolons, know everything
and remember how we struggled
to speak of life going by and how
difficult love is. Singing to themselves
they lightly slip a finger through the opening
in the world that mantles us
then pause, cheek pressed to the cat's ear
serious face turning blank so suddenly
it unsteadies us, pitches us beyond time,
dumbstruck as if beside a corpse-filled well
and meanwhile on the rim of our days,
of our pointless words, the cat's widening eyes.

Giacomo Leopardi

(*déchant*)

Ce n'est pas l'échelle de Jacob
cet escalier lustré du *Caffe Greco*
que la lune grimpe avec aisance
tandis qu'il souffle à chaque marche
plus pâle et voûté que son ombre.
L'ange froid de la gloire, il l'a vaincu
entre les pages des héros
mais ici que lui reste-t-il
à l'heure où la taverne rejoint la nuit:
trois boules de glace – fraise vanille pistache
que le regard seul entame et le désir plus fort
d'entendre encore une fois le cœur des jours anciens
résonner dans la coupelle de cristal.

Giacomo Leopardi

(descant)

It isn't Jacob's ladder
this glazed stairway to the *Caffe Greco*
where the moon climbs freely
while he wheezes with every step
more pale and stooped than his shadow.
He has trounced the cold angel of glory
amid the chronicled heroes
but what is left for him here
when the tavern rejoins the night:
three scoops of ice-cream – strawberry vanilla pistachio
tasted only by looking and the mounting urge
to hear once more the spirit of old times
ring in the crystal goblet.

Césare Pavese, 2

La fenêtre qui donne sur les quais
n'arrête pas la marche des trains
pas plus que la lumière n'arrête
la main qui tire les rideaux
tout juste si parfois du mur
un peu de plâtre se détache
un pétale touche le guéridon
il arrive aussi qu'un homme
laisse tomber son corps
sans réveiller personne

Césare Pavese, 2

The window looking out on the platforms
does not stop the movement of trains
any more than the light can stop
the hand drawing the curtains
and just as a bit of plaster
sometimes loosens from the wall
a petal brushes the iron table
so too a man
can let his body fall
and not wake anyone

La déchirure du ciel

(EXTRAIT)

IV

Et si le poème, c'était plus simplement
ce qui reste en souffrance dans la déchirure
du ciel, comme une valise sans couleur
un gant dans l'herbe – et le rayon de soleil
s'amuse avec les serrures, l'agrafe en fer blanc
cependant que nous restons en retrait
empêtrés dans nos ombres
comme un enfant grandi trop vite
et qui ne sait plus rire.

The Gap Between Clouds

(EXTRACT)

IV

And what if the poem were simply
whatever is left behind in the gap
between clouds, like a nondescript suitcase
a glove in the grass – the sun's ray
toying with the locks, the metal clasp
while we hang back
entangled in our shadows
like a child who has grown up too fast
and no longer laughs.

Hors de portée

Ah, s'il pouvait être de chair vivante, cet homme
debout sur l'horizon, qui charge les nuages
dans sa brouette, s'il pouvait emporter un peu
de la boue des jours qui traîne dans les regards
et les os, dissiper cette ombre en nous
qui fait tapisserie devant l'indéchiffrable
partition du ciel et de la terre,
tu ne piétinerais pas ici derrière la vitre
comme Jonas au fond du navire malmené,
priant que la lumière se fasse tout à coup
et que vibre l'accord de toutes choses:
désirs, joies, souffrances hors de portée
comme les voix blanches et noires de la musique.

Out of Reach

Ah, if only he were of living flesh, that man
who stands on the horizon loading clouds
into his barrow, if he could cart off some
of the days' sludge that lingers in eye
and bone, disperse this inward shadow of ours
left to itself before the unfathomable
orchestration of heaven and earth,
you wouldn't be here marking time behind the pane
like Jonah in the bowels of the buffeted ship,
praying for light to come breaking through
and for all things to sound in harmony:
desire, joy, suffering – out of reach
like music's white and black voices.

Février à vélo

(EXTRAIT)

I

Comme s'il fallait quand même croire un peu
à l'éternité qui se cache dans la doublure des vents,

j'ai serré, en bon cheval qui s'ignore,
mon désir de partir entre les dents

et pris mon vieux vélo, un habitué des caves
et arrière-boutiques puisque grand-père déjà

(mais c'est une autre histoire), en cordonnier habile,
utilisait la selle pour donner forme à des souliers.

Une fois lancé dans la descente, on oublie
que l'Histoire est du temps qui s'arrête

pour ramasser ses morts, et soi-même,
on se carre sur la machine pour passer

plus facilement entre les mailles
du présent qui résiste: ce poème promis,

stoppé au premier vers, la porte
du poulailler qui bâille et la liste

des courses pour le soir, dont le détail
se perd à mesure qu'on avance. Vite, un coup

de pédale et que l'oubli me prenne tout entier,
efface pour de bon le remords d'avoir fui

February on a Bike

(EXTRACT)

I

As if one needed a little faith, even so,
in eternity stowed in the lining of winds,

like a good horse that doesn't know it
I champed on the urge to be off and away

and took my old bike, a frequenter of cellars
and back-rooms since grandfather, being

an expert cobbler (but that's another story),
would use the saddle to form the shoes.

Launched on the downward slope, you forget
History is made of time that halts

to pick up its dead; and you, meanwhile,
astride the machine strike a pose to slip

more easily through the mesh
of the unyielding present: that promised poem,

stopped short at the first line, the door
of the hen-house left open and the list

of the evening's groceries, its details
vaguer the further you go. Quick, one thrust

on the pedals and may oblivion take me entire,
erasing for good all remorse at having fled

une chambre enfumée et clôturée de livres,
qu'il n'y ait plus à la fin pour signer mes papiers

qu'un paraphe de vent.

2

Et qu'importe la côte, et que le vélo grince
et que craquent les os: je suis parti et rien,
pas même la pluie qui gendarme le paysage

depuis dix jours pour avoir cru
au printemps avec deux mois d'avance, rien
ne découragera le fuyard surpris par son élan

comme un chaton retombant sur ses pattes
(pour un peu, il s'élancerait à nouveau dans le vide)
– surpris, dis-je, et qui s'en veut

d'être resté assis des heures en vain
à contempler sa feuille alors que le soleil
faisait le zouave à la fenêtre, tambourinant

– mais on est sourd aux signes d'allégresse
quand on baigne sans arrêt dans l'amère
illusion que tout est là entre les lignes

du papier: la vérité vraie et la vivante vie.
Qui s'en veut, oui, s'en veut de s'en vouloir
et voilà d'un seul coup la mécanique emballée

qui s'enraye (tout commence dans la tête,
disait l'autre, et finit dans le pédalier).
Pédaler, ne pas penser,

voilà bien la leçon.

a smoke-filled room walled in by books,
and may nothing be left to sign my papers

but a flourish of wind.

2

And so what if there's a hill, and the bicycle groans
and your bones are cracking: I'm off and nothing,
not even the rain that's bullied the countryside

ten days straight for believing
in spring two months too early, nothing
can daunt the runaway, surprised at his own impulse

like a kitten landing back on its feet
(given half a chance, he'd leap into thin air again)
– surprised, as I said, and cross with himself

for having sat all those hours in vain
contemplating the page while the sun
larked about at the window, playing tattoos

– but one is deaf to the sounds of joy
when you're always steeped in the bitter
illusion that everything's there between the lines

on the paper: the tangible truth, the lively life.
Cross with himself, yes, and cross at being cross
and all of a sudden the freewheeling mechanism

jams (everything starts in the head,
as they say, and ends up in the crank-gear).
Pedal hard, and no thinking,

that's surely the lesson.

La visite

Par la fenêtre entrouverte: mille cris d'oiseaux,
le vert bruissement et la voix d'une enfance
parmi les collines, l'assourdissante joie
de midi, voilà pour ce qui est de voir

et d'entendre, couché entre des draps blancs,
les porteurs d'oranges et de larmes rentrées
qui s'ingénient à doubler ton silence. La mer
tirant sur ses chaînes, c'est plus loin,

au fond des membres. Ici, à marée basse,
tu souris comme on aligne sur la plage
ces grands châteaux qui ne vieillissent pas:
ton cœur est dans la chambre haute,

qui voit de loin venir ce qu'il attend.

The Visit

Through the half-open window: a thousand bird-calls,
rustling green and the voice of a childhood
among the hills, the deafening jubilation
at midday, that's the sense of it, seeing

and hearing – as you lie between white sheets –
the bringers of oranges and choked-back tears
who contrive to imitate your silence. The sea
pulling on its chains is some way off

deep in the body's members. Here, at low tide,
you smile the way one builds on the beach
those rows of grand castles that never age:
your heart in the topmost chamber sees

far off the long-awaited, coming closer.

Un peu d'or dans la boue

(EXTRAIT)

VII

Si j'ai cherché – ai-je rien fait d'autre? –
ce fut comme on descend une rue en pente
ou parce que tout à coup les oiseaux
ne chantaient plus. Ce trou dans l'air,

entre les arbres, mon souffle ni mes yeux
ne l'ont comblé – et je criais souvent
au milieu des herbes, mais je n'attendais
rien, je me disais: voilà,

je suis au monde, le ciel est bleu, nuages
les nuages et qu'importe le cri sourd des pommes
sur la terre dure: la beauté, c'est que tout
va disparaître et que, le sachant,

tout n'en continue pas moins de flâner.

A Speck of Gold in the Mud

(EXTRACT)

VII

If I have searched – and what else have I done? –
I did so the way one walks down a sloping street
or because the birds stopped singing
all of a sudden. That hole in the air,

between the trees, which neither my breath nor my eyes
has ever filled in – and I'd often call out
as I stood in the grasses, though I expected
nothing, and I'd say to myself: look,

I'm in the world, the sky is blue, clouds
are clouds and what does it matter, that muffled cry
of apples on the hard ground: beauty means
it's all going to vanish and that, knowing this,

everything nonetheless idles along.

Partance

(EXTRAITS)

I

Au fond du jardin, il y avait la mer, c'est là que tout a commencé pour nous deux. Sans nous en douter le moins du monde: nous ne nous connaissions pas.

J'avais neuf, dix ans peut-être (je comptais mal ou je ne comptais pas, c'est un pli qui m'est resté, coûteux à la longue. On ne se refait pas).

Le jardin de mon père, ce que j'appelais ainsi, n'était pas un jardin, mais un grand morceau de terre constamment remuée. Cerné sur trois côtés de grosses fleurs multicolores, de groseilliers rouges et de cassis, il était fermé au bout par une rangée de peupliers. Brasseurs de ciel à longueur de jour, ces hauts arbres, par les nuits de grand vent, recrachaient la mer, la voix des sirènes et les chants des noyés.

J'étais seul à les entendre, il me semble, car mes parents refusaient de me croire et haussaient les épaules. Rien n'a changé depuis. […]

III

C'est ainsi que nous nous rencontrâmes, elle et moi, dans cet accablement où nous sombrions peu à peu, aboyant à la lune; elle, souffrant d'être attachée au piquet dans un paysage immobile; moi, d'être parti tant de fois pour revenir toujours au même endroit, à cette mer indéracinable au fond du jardin, si différente des mers que j'avais vues, et qui me parle comme personne, m'engageant sur des chemins qui n'ont pas où aller.

Là (je veux dire ici), nous l'avons amenée un beau matin (mais peut-être pleuvait-il), posée tout au bout d'un clos

Partance

(EXTRACTS)

I

At the end of the garden was the sea, where it all began for the two of us. Without our being the least aware: we did not yet know each other.

I was nine, maybe ten (I was bad at counting or didn't count at all, a failing that's stayed on and cost me dear in the long run. You are what you are).

My father's garden, as I called it, wasn't a garden but a large patch of earth that was constantly being dug over. Bordered on three sides by big, multi-coloured flowers, red-currants and black-currants, it was closed off at the end by a row of poplars. Stirring the sky all day long, these tall trees would, on blustery nights, spit back the sea and siren voices and the singing of the drowned.

I was the only one to hear them, it seems, as my parents refused to believe me and simply shrugged. Nothing has changed since. [...]

III

That was how we met, she and I, in a despondency that had us sinking by degrees, howling at the moon; she, from being tethered in an unmoving landscape; I, from having gone away so often and each time come back to the same place, to that unbudgeable sea at the end of the garden, so different from the seas I had known, speaking to me like no one else, inviting me down roads that have nowhere to go.

It is there (by which I mean here) that we brought her one fine morning (though perhaps it was raining), and put her at the far end of a plot more or less like the plot in my childhood. For I had meanwhile grown up, left father and

pareil à peu de chose près au clos de mon enfance. Car j'avais grandi entre-temps, quitté père et mère, fondé famille et tiré pour mes enfants une maison de la terre, un peu comme font les taupes, m'enfonçant jour après jour plus profond dans les galeries du devoir quotidien et des soucis.

La caravane m'a sauvé. Derrière un verger planté de «basses-tiges» – tous arbres à fruits, même le cerisier qui n'a jamais donné que des merles – qui masquaient à ma vue la maison pleine de fureur et de bruits, j'avais enfin trouvé un lieu à ma mesure, entre le camp volant et la cabane dans les branches, entre départ et arrivée.

Je la baptisai *Partance*.

IV

Le jardin en septembre a l'air d'un cimetière, avec ses touffes de verdure, deçà delà, ses fruits tombés et qui pourrissent, ses herbes folles, montées en graines, séchées sur pied; et la tache blanche derrière les arbres qui s'époumonent à retenir leurs feuilles, n'est-ce pas exactement la chemise du gardien qui fume dans le soir tombant? Sa porte longtemps reste ouverte sur les framboisiers qui envahissent, et sur les ronces.

Le jour peut s'en aller, la nuit: nous ne nous quitterons pas. Partance vieillira, verdira lentement, sifflera de plus en plus fort dans les grands vents, s'endormira avec la pluie, partira de nouveau. Ce sera par un jour de nuages noirs, et dans la bousculade. En attendant, s'enraciner lui sera doux comme une sagesse. Mourir est-ce rien d'autre que l'apprentissage d'un langage nouveau, la modulation infinie du verbe partir quand il ne se conjugue plus?

Je me ferai petit pour apprendre avec elle, de l'intérieur, comment doubler le cap des illusions et atteindre, au large, à cette vie entrevue dans le jardin d'enfance.

mother, founded a family and heaved up an earth house for my children, rather as moles do, plunging day after day ever more deeply into the galleries of routine duty and worries.

The caravan saved me. Behind an orchard planted with "short-trunked" varieties – all fruit trees, even the cherry that yields only blackbirds – which hid from view the rage-filled, noisy house, I had at last found a place whose measure was mine, between tent and tree-house, departure and arrival.

I baptized her *Partance*.

IV

The garden in September looks like a cemetery, with its clumps of greenery here and there, its fallen fruit rotting, its weeds running to seed and drying out where they stand; and the white blob behind trees breathlessly clinging on to their leaves, surely that's the shirt of the caretaker who's out in the gathering dusk having a smoke? For a long while his door is left open on the encroaching raspberry bushes, and the brambles.

Let the days go by, and the nights: we will not leave one another. Partance will grow old and slowly turn green, her whistling steadily shriller in the strong winds; she'll fall asleep with the rain and will be on her way once more. It'll be on a day of black clouds, all helter-skelter. Meanwhile, putting down roots will delight her, much as wisdom itself. What is dying, if not an apprenticeship to a new language, the infinite modulation of the verb "to leave", when the conjugating falters?

I will be humble and learn with her, from the inside, how to weather the cape of illusions and – in the open sea – catch up with life as glimpsed in that childhood garden.

V

Avant que tout s'en aille comme c'est venu, car tout s'en va et les meilleures choses ont une fin, dit-on; avant que s'achève notre bout de chemin ensemble, Partance et moi, dire ce qu'elle est simplement avec des mots qui s'en iront eux aussi, un jour, comme le reste. Décrire est un acte d'amour, disait un poète.

L'intérieur est modeste comme une cabine de pilotage, quatre mètres sur deux, mais je compte mal, je l'ai dit, et l'enthousiasme n'arrange rien. Mettons trois sur un et demi, au décimètre près. En tout cas, qui suffit bien à mon désir. Côté verger, une banquette étroite pour la sieste; côté prairies, deux autres avec coussins, et une table pliante qui sert à les réunir en un lit confortable. Au milieu de la cloison latérale qui regarde la porte, un évier en aluminium surmonté d'une étagère. J'y rangerai quelques livres, les indispensables, pas plus d'une dizaine, de quoi rêver longtemps.

La lumière du jour entre par quatre baies, à profusion: pare-brise avant, lunette arrière comme en voiture, et deux petites latérales à rideaux. Décentrée au plafond, une lucarne à tabatière. Voilà mon île au milieu des champs, avec le ciel par-dessus.

Là-bas, derrière les arbres, la maison déjà s'enfonce, où j'aime à croire qu'on m'a oublié, tout rassuré qu'on est de me savoir à deux pas. Mais je suis loin et une mer nous sépare que nul ne voit.

Bientôt, on n'entend plus que la hulotte là-haut sur la colline boisée. Les chiens se sont tus et la caravane passe lentement, comme remorquée par le nuage rouge qui descend la vallée.

V

Before everything goes the way it came, for all of it will go, and all good things come to an end, as they say; before this journey we've shared is over for Partance and me, I'll say something about her in simple words that will also go one day, like everything else. Describing is an act of love, to quote a poet.

The interior is modest, like a cockpit, four metres by two, though as I've said, I'm not good at figures, and enthusiasm doesn't help. Let's say three by one-and-a-half, give or take a decimetre. In any case, I wouldn't wish for more. On the orchard side, a narrow seat for afternoon rests; on the meadows side, two more with cushions, and a folding table that brings them together to make a single comfortable bed. In the middle of the side wall, opposite the door, an aluminium sink with shelves above it. I'll put some books there, the essential ones, not more than about ten, for something to dream on at leisure.

Daylight comes through four bay-windows, pouring in: a front windscreen and a back window, as in a car, and two small side-windows with curtains. Off-centre in the ceiling, a hinged skylight. Here it is, my island among the fields, with the sky above.

Over there, behind the trees, the house is already sinking, and I'd like to think they've forgotten me, assured as they are to know I'm close by. But I am a long way off, and between us lies a sea no one has noticed.

Soon there is nothing to be heard but the hoot-owl up there on the wooded hill. The dogs have fallen quiet and the caravan passes slowly, as if towed by the reddish cloud moving away down the valley.

Variations sur une montée en tramway

(d'après une photo de J.-H. Lartigue, 1900)

I

Assis à l'arrière, à contre-sens et fumaillant
dans le jour frais, il a vivement tourné la tête

vers l'inconnue qui sautait dans le tramway
en marche, une main relevant la jupe et

découvrant le mollet rond et la cheville
serrés dans le bas noir. Il a tout vu, tout

senti, tout entendu: la vivacité de l'ablette
dans le courant, la saveur du premier

fruit dérobé à l'étalage, et comme
la verge de coudrier sifflait dans l'air

quand elle allait s'abattre sur son dos
d'enfant, mais à l'heure de parler d'elle

aux amis curieux et qui riaient d'avance,
plus rien, ni grâce, ni éclat, mais des mots

comme les papiers gras sur l'herbe après la fête,
quand l'ombre s'allonge et nous glace le cœur.

II

Le contrôleur n° 559, n'a vu que le danger
encouru par la belle et déjà sa main droite

Variations on a Tram Ride

(after a photo by J.-H. Lartigue, 1900)

I

Sitting at the rear, facing backwards and having a smoke
in the brisk air, he turned round sharply

as the unknown woman leapt aboard
the moving tram, one hand hitching her skirt and

revealing a shapely calf and ankle
snug in a black stocking. He saw everything, felt

everything, heard it all: the liveliness of minnows
in a current, the taste of the first

fruit thieved from the market stall, and how
the hazel switch whistled in the air

just before it came down on his young
back, though when the time came to speak of it

to curious friends already giggling,
nothing was left, neither grace nor sparkle, just words

like greasy wrappers on the grass after festivals,
when shadows lengthen, chilling our hearts.

II

Conductor no. 559 has seen only the danger
facing the belle and already his right hand

a lâché l'ombre pour la proie. Trop tard,
l'intrépide est à bord, un pied sur la marche,

l'autre encore dans le vide, traînant
la pointe de l'escarpin sur la terre qui bouge.

C'est assez pour que le voyageur se retourne,
remonte la couture du bas jusqu'à la nuque

d'herbe tendre que broute un chapeau cloche.
S'il sut jamais rien du visage d'albâtre,

de la bouche cerise et des yeux agrandis,
il emporta cela qui fait battre longtemps

le sang des choses comme un cœur
dans l'ombre des chambres mortes:

l'effroi de la rose ébouriffée, la cendre
de toutes les promesses dans le tiroir

du temps, la mort qui vient
à notre rencontre et ne se retourne pas.

has let go the shadow for the catch itself. Too late.
Intrepid, she's now on board, one foot on the step,

the other still in the air, dragging
the toe of her pump on the moving ground.

It's enough to make the passenger turn round,
ascend the seam of her stocking to the nape

with its tender grass where a cloche hat browses.
Even knowing nothing of the alabaster face,

the cherry mouth and the widened eyes,
he took with him something that makes

the blood of things pulse on, like a heart
in the shadow of deadened rooms:

the fright of the dishevelled rose, the ash
of all promises left in the drawer

of time, and death which is coming
to meet us and will not turn back.

Envoi

Je me souviens comme l'enfant tirait sa mère
par le bras, à gauche à droite: un vrai petit
cheval de cirque, et comme elle

continuait sa marche, fière et sourde statue
dont la tête coupée dans un autre temps
avait roulé parmi les fruits, les légumes,

dans le panier accroché à sa main
avec les projets, les amours, les mille et une
nuits d'attente rangés sur l'étagère invisible

qu'elle comptait, recomptait des lèvres.
Et lui tirait et sa mère résistait, sachant bien
de quelle valeur sont les ailes

confectionnées dans l'ombre avec des bouts
de ficelle et des plumes d'édredon,
et de combien leur poids dépasse un espoir

d'homme dans la balance des vents,
elle qui, tant et tant de fois déjà,
derrière les persiennes de sa chambre,

enfanta Icare en criant.

Envoi

I remember how the child used to pull his mother
by the arm, left and right: a proper little
circus pony, and how she would

keep on walking, a deaf, dignified statue
whose head, severed in a bygone time,
had rolled among the fruits and vegetables,

in the basket hooked on her arm
with the plans, the loves, the thousand and one
nights of waiting laid out on the invisible dresser

for her to count, count again on her lips.
And he'd pull and his mother would resist, knowing well
the value of wings when they're

made in the shadows with bits
of string and eiderdown feathers,
and how their weight exceeds mortal

hope in the balance of the winds,
she who so many, many times before
in her shuttered room had given

birth to Icarus amid her cries.

L'adieu

Tu peux bien prendre la mer par les cheveux
et la secouer comme un vieux tapis,
endormir toute une forêt en la regardant
droit dans les yeux, attacher

le vent au bout d'une ficelle et le mener
à la baguette, c'est facile, à peine
un jeu d'enfant dans la chambre des mots
et l'univers dans ta poche n'est plus

qu'une bille de verre, mais effacer une lettre,
une seule, du cri qu'elle a poussé
quand, brûlant ses derniers vaisseaux,
tu as laissé retomber sur le seuil

sa main blanche, ça non.

The Adieu

You can grab the sea by the hair
and shake it like an old carpet,
put a whole forest to sleep by staring
it straight in the eye, fasten

the wind to a string and rule it
with a rod of iron, it's easy, barely
child's play in a roomful of words
and the universe in your pocket's no more

than a marble, but to erase one letter,
even one, from the cry she uttered
when, burning her last boats,
you stood on the threshold and let go

her white hand – that, no.

Gilles Ortlieb

GILLES ORTLIEB was born in 1953 in Morocco, where he spent a good part of his childhood. His father was a doctor and his mother an avant-garde painter. The family returned to Paris, and Gilles Ortlieb studied Classics at the Sorbonne. After a year of military service, recorded in his first prose text, *Soldats et autres récits* (Le temps qu'il fait, 1991), the poet was diversely employed (puppeteer, night-porter in a small Parisian hotel) and earned money to travel widely in the Mediterranean. His love of Greece and Greek language and culture dates from the 1970s, and found its first fruition in an edition of Cavafy's poems (co-translated with Pierre Leyris), first published by Seghers in 1978, with a revised, expanded edition in 1987. His first collection of poems, *Brouillard journalier* (1984), introduced a subtle new voice, discreet, melancholic, gently humorous, deeply attentive to the events and mood-changes of the quotidian. In 1986, Ortlieb took up a post at the European Union translation agency, based in Luxembourg. Since that time, he has found in the *Petit-Duché de Luxembourg*, or the *Gibraltar du Nord*, as he called his subsequent collections (Le temps qu'il fait, 1991, 1995), a major source of inspiration, which is based on the bitter-sweetness of exile, its mixture of *spleen* and strangeness. In frequent *sorties* with notebook Ortlieb has chronicled the sights and sounds of neighbouring Lorraine, with its disused steelworks and depressed towns. His main collections of poetry and prose (culled from his *carnets*) include *La Nuit de Moyeuvre* (2000), *Carnets de ronde* (2004), *Meuse Métal, etc.* (2005), *Sous le crible* (2008). In addition, Ortlieb has published two volumes of critical essays, *Sept petites études* (2002) and *Des orphelins* (2007). A memorable study of Baudelaire's last years in Belgium, *Au Grand Miroir*, came out in 2005. Ortlieb has continued to publish translations from Greek, notably texts by George Seferis, Mikhaïl Mitsakis and Thanassis Valtinos. In 2002, his earlier poems were collected by Gallimard in *Place au cirque*.

Les mauvaises soirées

autrement dit où l'on ne sort guère de soi
et encore moins de chez soi, dans le seul
véhicule d'une paire de sandales fanées
pour arpenter le territoire et ses confins,
reprendre l'un ou l'autre livre en main
sans en élire aucun, tâcher de combler
les retards du courrier puis y renoncer
quelques lignes plus loin – en résumé,
où l'on renâcle, insatisfait, à mi-chemin
entre faim et satiété, incapable pourtant
de nommer cela qui persiste à manquer.
Des phrases ou bris de vers affleurent ici
et là, qui ne laisseront que leurs miettes
à ramasser, comme brins de tabac guidés
du tranchant de la main vers la corbeille
à papier. Et la pensée se berce dans ce va-
et-vient, tâtonne vers son nadir jusqu'à
ce que l'heure nous enjoigne de dormir
– et de se débarrasser enfin des sandales
sans âge: les idées, aussitôt, s'allègent,
grimpent à l'assaut d'abrupts raidillons
puis s'égaillent par des sentiers volages.
La soirée, finalement, n'était pas si ratée:
mieux, on se surprend même à souhaiter
qu'elles puissent toutes lui ressembler:
ne finirait-on pas, tôt ou tard, par avancer?

Bad Evenings

meaning those when you barely emerge from
yourself, let alone the house, with nothing
but a pair of faded sandals by way of transport
as you pace the territory to its limits, pick up one
or other of your current books without deciding
between them, tackle the pile of waiting letters
then give up after a few lines – in short,
when you dither, dissatisfied, somewhere
between hunger and repleteness, yet cannot
put your finger on what is missing.
Here and there a phrase crops up, remnants
of lines, and all they will leave is scattered
crumbs, like the shreds of tobacco your hand
sweeps towards the waste-paper basket.
And thought, lulled by these comings
and goings, gropes towards its nadir
until time insists that we go to sleep
– and kick off the ageless sandals
at last: which is when, suddenly, ideas
find a lightness, go charging up slopes
then scatter away along flighty paths.
The evening was not, after all, a write-off;
better still, you find yourself wishing
they were all like that: wouldn't you finally,
sooner or later, make some headway?

Un geste

infime, et ancien, que celui consistant à appuyer le dos
de la cuillère tout contre le bord du bol ou de l'assiette
à soupe pour empêcher celle-ci de goutter sur le trajet
de la bouche; rite sonore, à peine, lesté par une longue
pratique dans l'enclos de cuisines trop ou mal éclairées,
dans le périmètre des campagnes sourdes ou banlieues
verticales, à l'écart: geste de femme ou d'homme seuls
sous le plafonnier, de pensées ralenties revenant buter
sur l'obstacle de penser quand la main, suivant la courbe,
s'abaisse un peu vers la fin, dans l'assentiment d'exister.

The Act

tiny, and venerable, consists of running the back
of the spoon across the rim of the plate or soup bowl
so it won't drip on its way to the mouth, a faintly
resonant ritual solemnized by long observance
in the interiors of over- or under-lit kitchens
in deadened rural precincts or cut-off vertical
suburbs: the act of a solitary man or woman
under a ceiling lamp, sluggish thoughts coming
back to bump against the obstacle to their thinking
when the hand, following the curve, dips slightly
right before the last moment, existence reconfirmed.

Café de l'Usine

Usines à froid, usines à chaud et *Grands Bureaux*
entre Fameck et Hayange. Y tombent à l'oblique,
au-dessus des voies ferrées, buses et corbeaux
parmi les reliques d'un Noël ancien, ampoules
cassées. D'étranges lichens aux teintes soufrées
envahissent les terre-pleins sous le ciel normal
et bleu, encore tramé par les tuyères abolies
des hauts-fourneaux; plus loin, l'usine à rails
qui, pour avoir tant dérouillé, peut enfin se laisser
rouiller, paisible, dans la campagne recouvrée.

Café de l'Usine

Cold steelworks, hot steelworks and *Head Offices*
between Fameck and Hayange. Slanting down
over the rail-tracks come crows and buzzards
among the relics of some Christmas, smashed
light-bulbs. Strange sulphurous-tinted lichens
invade the embankments under an ordinary
blue sky, still criss-crossed with disused
blast-pipes from the furnaces; further off
the rail-forging factory, having done so much
work unrusting can now, in peace at last
where the countryside has resumed, rust over.

Février

Neige éparse et distraite, à peine
lestée du poids de l'air lui-même
parmi le volettement des odeurs
de givre et d'industrie ancienne.
Feuilles remuées dans les angles
morts comme coques d'insectes
séchés, terre gelée et dimanche
dormant, assiégé par les freux,
à tisonner entre cendres et feu.

February

Sparse and scattered snow, barely
filled with the weight of air itself
amid the cross-flitter of smells,
antiquated industry and frost.
Stirrings of leaves in the dead
corners like desiccated insect
shells, earth frozen and Sunday
asleep, besieged by rooks,
to be poked between ash and fire.

Petite ville aux reflets de houille et d'étain,
aux arbres morts plantés vifs sur les remparts,
hautes radiographies de poumons sur fond
de ciel éteint. Et l'on voudrait douter
de ce que l'on voit, comme de la combe
ouverte devant soi, entre les collets posés
des sentiers anciens et les leurres de demain,
au chiffre introuvé. Ne demander qu'un peu
de lumière, de calme intérieur, pour les heures
à venir et la nuit qui suivra: petite loque
de prière serrée entre les dents, gardée.

Small town with its gleams of coal and tin,
its dead trees planted alive on the ramparts,
magnified lungs in X-ray on a background
of dull sky. And you would rather not believe
what you see, like the valley open before you,
between the sprung traps of the old paths
and the snares of tomorrow, their number
undiscovered. Ask for no more than a little
light, some inner calm, for the hours ahead
and the night after that: this shred of prayer
clenched between your teeth, and holding.

Neige à Thionville, lumières petites, lumières,
salles à manger, appentis, cuisines éclairées,
maisons basses et jardinets, un instant cachés
par les flancs d'un convoi de la «Transcéréalière».
Feux mobiles, lancés dans l'obscurité et déjà éteints:
passage sans traces, pour peu que le train accélère
à nouveau et glisse, comme devant, sur les bords
d'une campagne gelée, pour filer une fois encore
vers l'est et le néant, en égrenant sans bruit
les nœuds de l'écheveau.

Snow in Thionville, small lights, lights,
dining-rooms, wallpapers, bright kitchens,
low houses and garden plots, briefly eclipsed
by the convoy of the Transcéréalière freight.
Moving lamps cast into the dark, extinguished:
no trace left as the train begins to pick up speed
again and slides past frozen country, heading
once more for the east and nothingness, silently
counting the knots along the skein.

La brume a dissimulé la brume qui cache les trois lumières,
posées à ras de l'eau, du café de *Jean le Pauvre*. Du fleuve
jauni pendant la nuit dernière, le débit ne cesse plus d'enfler
et c'est tout un paysage noyé qui tressaille au passage
des trente-neuf (je le sais pour les avoir parfois comptés)
wagons des mines, vision pareille et neuve dans le dérèglement
continu de la mécanique intime. La part de l'ombre
ne se laissera plus, ce soir, apprivoiser: n'importe,
sortir et assouplir encore, par un dernier tour, la phrase
de peu de secours.

The mist has concealed the mist that hides the three lights
level with the water at the café *Jean le Pauvre.* The river
turned yellow in the night, its flow steadily swelling
and a whole drowned landscape trembles at the passing
of the thirty-nine (I've counted) waggons from the mines,
the same and brand-new vision in the constant disarray
of inner workings. Tonight the dark side will not let itself
be tamed: no matter, take a last turn outside, exercise
words that bring small comfort.

Déménager

(EXTRAIT)

Du fond de ces semaines peu ou mal éclairées qui auront pourtant renvoyé à plus noir que soi, où l'œil et l'esprit venaient très assidûment se poser sur la flamme d'un soldat inconnu tremblotant de l'autre côté d'un pont aux piles podagres; durant ces nuits suréclairées par le sodium orangé d'un réverbère fiché juste devant la fenêtre, si puissant qu'il illuminait, les soirs de neige, les flocons par transparence, au point que je pouvais me croire pris – ce qui est plus d'une fois arrivé – dans le tourbillon artificiel d'un presse-papiers en plastique qu'on vient d'agiter. Au besoin, je pourrai lire sans allumer la lampe.

Voisinage: un marchand de journaux arménien, aussi renfrogné que sa femme, par compensation, est souriante, un sex-shop annonçant 3000 programmes à la carte et trois spécialités qui s'allument la nuit en lettres jaunes sur fond rouge (*Leder*, *Lack*, *Latex* – si je vois à peu près ce qu'il en est du cuir et du latex, la laque, en revanche, m'intrigue) et dont je n'ai jamais vu sortir, un après-midi, l'air dégagé, qu'un labrador au poil crème, deux boutiques de retouches (*Maxi-retouches* et une nouvelle venue, *Family Retouche*, que *Maxi-retouches* n'a pas dû voir s'installer d'un très bon œil), une horlogerie-bijouterie le plus souvent déserte, un coiffeur nommé Fernand, un magasin, condamné par sa désuétude même, *Électro-Viaduc*, et un *pastificio bolognese*. De bonne réputation.

S'habituer aux bruits nouveaux: les talons du dessus, la porte d'en dessous, le piano d'à côté, les stores d'en face, les ahans s'échappant en fin de journée d'un gymnase proche. Se déplacer d'un appartement à l'autre, d'un quartier à un autre, comme une façon de ruser entre les différents étages de soi.

Moving

(EXTRACT)

Out of the depths of these weeks, barely or poorly lit, which nonetheless pointed to somewhere darker than the self, where eye and mind settled assiduously on the flame of the unknown soldier flickering on the far side of a bridge set on gouty piles; through these nights lit by the over-bright orange of a sodium streetlamp planted right in front of the window, so powerful that on snowy evenings it shone in the flakes' transparency, till it was easy to believe I was caught – as I have been more than once – in the whirl of artificial snow shaken in a plastic paperweight. If I wanted, I could read without switching on the lamp.

In the neighbourhood: an Armenian newsagent, as sullen as his wife – to balance things up – is sunny; a sex shop announcing 3,000 programmes to choose from and three specialities that light up at night in yellow letters on a red background (*Leder, Lack, Latex* – while I can more or less visualize the business with leather and latex, the lacquer remains intriguing) from which I have never seen a soul emerge except, one afternoon, a cream-coloured Labrador looking rather perky; two seamstresses (*Maxi-retouches,* and a newcomer, *Family Retouche,* whose opening cannot have been welcomed by *Maxi-retouches*); a watch-and-jewellery shop for the most part deserted; a hairdresser called Fernand; a shop, *Électro-Viaduc,* condemned by its own desuetude, and a *pastificio bolognese.* Of good repute.

Getting used to new noises: the heels upstairs, the door down below, the neighbour's piano, the blinds opposite, the grunts coming from a nearby gym at the end of the day. Moving from flat to flat, from district to district, as if to outwit the different storeys of the self.

Refusant de «s'installer», on passe son temps à ça, s'installer.

Et toujours cette vulnérabilité de bernard-l'hermite délogé. Aucun progrès à cet égard, on ne s'aguerrit pas. Tout au plus apprend-on à se perfectionner dans l'art de remplir les caisses de livres qui s'entassent dans les pièces à quitter, les cages d'escalier respectives, les pièces à aménager. Existence emballée, stockée, transbahutée, chiffrable en nombre de cartons.

Refusing to "settle down", one spends all one's time doing just that, "settling down".

And always this vulnerability, like an evicted hermit-crab. No progress there, one never toughens up. At most, you come to perfect the art of packing books into boxes that pile up in rooms to be vacated, on the old and the new landings, in the rooms to be organized. An existence packaged, stocked, carted about, quantifiable in the number of boxes.

Ode (pour traverser les jours sans maugréer)

à la petite tasse émaillée, au rebord bleuté,
dont le métal brûle lorsque, par distraction,
on la saisit non par l'anse, mais par les côtés.
Compagne des débuts de nuit et des travaux
en cours, jamais très éloignée du *Nouveau
dictionnaire analogique* de Niobey sur quoi
il lui arrive d'être posée – et qui veille seule
au milieu des objets, à la température exacte
de la pièce, avant de resservir le lendemain
et les lendemains des lendemains, intacte.

Ode (for getting through the days without grumbling)

to the small enamel mug edged in blue
and its metal that burns if you seize it
distractedly by the sides, not the handle.
Companion of night-time drafts, of works
in progress, never too far from the Niobey
Nouveau dictionnaire analogique on which
it is sometimes placed – it sits on alone
among other objects, exactly at the temperature
of the room, to be used next morning and
mornings after the mornings after, unscathed.

Décembres

(EXTRAITS)

VOICI PLUSIEURS jours, en somme, que j'observe
dans un rayon variable, qui va de l'encadrement
de la fenêtre aux grands axes et ruelles alentour,
la réinstallation des guirlandes dans les arbres,
sur les grues, les façades, sans pouvoir congédier
l'impression très tenace qu'il s'agit là de tessons
pour la vue, d'angles vifs et blessants dans le noir
prégnant, de barbelés lumineux en quelque sorte,
aussi peu faits pour allumer l'idée d'une fête au-
dessus des passants qu'un morceau de corde posé
sur la table d'un pendu récent. (J'exagère, sûrement;
il n'empêche, comment désactiver pour soi-même
cette électricité veuve, aux entrelacs clignotants?)

Decembers

(EXTRACTS)

FOR SEVERAL days now, in short, I have watched
in varying arcs from the window-frame
to the major thoroughfares and side-streets,
Christmas wreaths being reinstalled on trees
on cranes, house-fronts, and I can't shake off
the stubborn impression that these are so many
shards to snag the gaze, sharp-angled and wounding
in the gravid dark, a kind of luminous barbed wire
as unlikely to inspire festive thoughts in passers-by
below as a piece of rope laid on the table of a man
just hanged. (I exaggerate, true, but how to disconnect
it for oneself, this bereft voltage blinking on and off?)

DÉCEMBRE, mois entre tous malcommode
à dire, à raison de ce qu'il célèbre, exhibe
en le cachant, tient enfoui sous l'enfance
et ses âges, entre potlatch et renoncement.
D'où, sans doute, ce presque soulagement
de l'heure première, à l'instant de quitter
la nuitée intime et ses amonts incertains,
pour une aube extérieure balisée de lueurs,
réverbères, trottoirs vivants. La journée,
au su et au vu de tous aiguise ses pointes
et ses stylets, ou bien dispose ses édredons,
plis d'oreiller, nuages courbes, c'est selon.

DECEMBER, the month most awkward of all
to describe, seeing what is celebrated
and displayed by hiding it, stowed beneath
childhood in all its stages, between potlatch
and turning away. Which probably explains
the near-consolation of early hours, the moment
one leaves the secret night-shift with its dubious
upper reaches, for a dawn marked out in lights,
streetlamps, pavements with signs of life. The day,
as everyone plainly knows, sharpens its spikes
and its knives, or else arranges its eiderdowns
and creased pillows, rounded clouds, depending.

Veille de veille de Noël dans l'Est, cette année encore, et repas de fête annoncé à la brasserie de la place Wallis, qui offre quelques chambres en étage à de jeunes émigrées russes en transit: le 24 décembre à 20 heures, *Traïpen mat Äppel* (*boudin aux pommes*) et vin mousseux; la télé, continûment branchée sur un canal animalier, y déroulera pour rien des reportages nombreux sur les mœurs des hyènes, la toilette des grands félins, la chasse à l'éléphant ou le déplacement des oursins. En regard de la place, pour animer le tableau, *La Maison du Diabète*, une taverne de l'Aiglon à l'enseigne désuète et, contrastant avec la boutique de régime voisine, les néons du cabaret *Coyote Girls* pourvoyant à l'envi promesses de spectacles et de divertissement.

Eve of Christmas Eve in the east, this year too,
and there's a festive meal to be had at the Brasserie
on the Place Wallis, which rents out upper rooms
to young Russian emigrées passing through:
24th December 8 p.m., *Traïpen mat Äppel*
(black pudding with apple) and sparkling wine;
the TV will be set to a wildlife channel reporting
for no one on the habits of hyenas, the cleaning rituals
of the great cats, elephant-hunting, or how sea-urchins
move. Viewed from the square, the scene is enlivened
by the Diabetics' Centre, a tavern under the quaint sign
of the Eaglet, and by way of contrast with the next-door
slimming boutique, the neon of the *Coyote Girls* cabaret,
supplying shows and entertainments a go–go.

PAR LA FENÊTRE, un petit homme en cache-col bronze et chapeau de feutre grisâtre, flanqué d'un quadrupède au poil plus miel que roux, et qui escorte chacun de ses pas. L'étonnant est que tous les deux s'immobilisent parfois longuement, malgré le froid, pour ausculter le ciel ou en dévisager les abords immédiats, regardant passer les voitures et les suivant des yeux jusqu'au tournant, puis pivotant de trois-quarts pour jouir d'un autre angle de vue, avant – à l'issue d'une station plus prolongée encore que d'habitude (admirable patience du chien, qui feint de s'intéresser aussi à ce presque rien dont il est témoin) – de se résigner à rentrer, à pas prudents que le verglas étrécit. Et quand on les croit disparus, ils sont là de nouveau, en faction, l'homme au couvre-chef gris et son renard miniature au poil plus blond que roux, qui emboîte chaque demi-pas de son compagnon.

THROUGH THE WINDOW, a small man in a tan scarf
and grey felt hat, flanked by a quadruped
more honey-colour than russet, who escorts
his every step. The astonishing thing is how
the two of them sometimes stop dead for long
intervals, despite the cold, to listen closely
to the sky or stare at the scene around them,
gazing after cars until they've turned the corner
then swivelling round three-quarters to enjoy
another angle of vision, until – emerging from
an even longer pause than usual (the admirable
patience of the dog as he feigns interest
in the virtual non-events he is witness to)
– they resign themselves to going back home,
the hard frost shrinking their pace to careful steps.
And when you think they have gone, there they are
again, in league, grey-hatted man, his diminutive fox
with a coat more blond than russet, treading
in the prints of his companion's every half-stride.

ARRIÈRE-COUR EN HIVER, avec fumées montant
droites contre un ciel couleur chair, et clartés
tamisées sur les façades voisines, sans aucun
des tressautements colorés par les téléviseurs:
le lait de cette Nativité n'en sera pas tourné.
Une soirée tranquille, en somme, pour relire
Cendrars, Strindberg, ou quelque prosateur
d'Europe centrale à peu près ignoré. La neige
tombée hier sur le balcon s'est recroquevillée
avec d'infimes crissements (mais quel travail
du gel saura tenir compagnie en suffisance?).
Un rectangle d'étoiles se déplace de guingois
entre les toitures, flocons de sel sur du papier
huilé, à la trajectoire millimétrée: une bonace
nocturne, pour ainsi dire, nimbant sans effort
le mobilier perché des antennes et cheminées.
L'inquiétude est, pour l'heure, lac peu visible
d'ici, à la surface sombre et qui ne tremble pas.

BACK-YARD IN WINTER, smoky plumes climbing
straight up against a flesh-coloured sky, and light
filtered to gleams on the facing walls, with none
of the tinted flickering cast by televisions sets:
this Nativity's milk will not be soured by them.
All in all, a quiet evening on which to re-read
Cendrars, Strindberg, or some almost unheard-of
proser from Central Europe. Yesterday's snow
on the balcony has shrunk in a series of crisp, tiny
creakings (but then how hard a frost would it take
to be really companionable?). A skewed rectangle
of stars has come down between the roofs, flecks
of salt on oil-coated paper, traced to the nearest
millimetre: a nocturnal lull, so to speak, giving
an easy halo to fittings of aerials and chimneypots.
Anxiety is, for now, a lake that's barely visible
from here, its surface dark and untrembling.

LA SAISON SE DÉSINCARCÈRE de la saison, à reculons, les traînées de sel semblent maintenant l'emporter en quantité sur la neige lorsque celle-ci, devenue motteuse et grisâtre, s'efforce malgré tout de durer dans l'air adouci, en monticules ternes et racornis qui rappelleraient assez des cadavres de hérissons. Ou bien s'aplatit à l'écart en plaques goudronnées, par l'ombre sauvées; quelques jours après la chute, les derniers cristaux encore immaculés sont ceux qu'on aperçoit sous les algues, à l'étal des écaillers – et qu'ils s'apprêtent à jeter au caniveau, une fois les festivités passées.

HALTINGLY SEASON UNSHACKLES itself from season,
the salt trails already more plentiful than the snow,
it seems, though the latter, now grey and lumpy,
still tries to survive in the softer air, its dull
hard heaps looking not unlike dead hedgehogs.
Or else it is flattened aside in asphalt sheets
saved by the shade; a few days after the snowfall,
the last immaculate crystals are the ones you notice
under the seaweed on the oyster-sellers' stalls
– and they will be dumped in the gutter once
the merriment is done.

Pour un portrait de Saxl

(EXTRAITS)

Melancolia è una ninfa gentile ... Et il avait dit cela d'un ton un peu absent mais tranquille, presque serein, comme il avait un autre jour déclaré regarder par la fenêtre le «destin de la pluie», ou comme on caresserait distraitement les flancs d'un chien endormi. Ne m'avait-il pas répliqué une fois, alors que je lui conseillais de participer le moins possible à la vie de l'Agence, puisqu'elle semble lui être devenue si pénible, de faire le mort dans son bureau: «Mais je n'ai pas besoin de faire semblant, je le suis, mort... ».

Parfois, il me vient de le comparer à une surface mate, à la capacité d'imprégnation infinie, et qui ne réfléchirait qu'une infime partie de ce qu'elle absorbe. Un puits sans fond, que ne parviendront jamais à combler les lectures les plus diverses, les plus contradictoires, de ses dimanches sans tain: d'un chapelet de romans policiers aux écrits de Lie Tseu, en passant par tel ouvrage savant sur les motifs des tapis orientaux ou l'obscure biographie d'un petit maître viennois.

L'appelant un soir chez lui:
— Je te dérange? Tu étais en train de dîner?
— Moi, dîner? Je «dîne», comme tu dis, très rarement. Non, je mange debout, comme les chevaux...

Derrière son visage lisse, glabre, reposé le plus souvent, quels remous et tourbillons dégénérant parfois en quel carnage intime et quotidien? Ce qu'il avait un jour appelé, d'une façon que j'avais trouvée, sans le lui dire, assez maniérée (mais peut-être ne pensait-il pas tant à lui-même qu'aux quatre murs de son bureau, où nous nous trouvions) «le petit théâtre des métamorphoses», sous-entendant sans doute «vers le pire». Mais quelle paix aussi, sûrement, certains jours.

Sketches for a Portrait of Saxl

(EXTRACTS)

Melancolia è une ninfa gentile... And he had said that in a rather absent-minded tone, almost serenely, as he had on another day declared himself to be looking at the "destiny of the rain", or as one might pensively stroke the flanks of a sleeping dog. Had he not once responded, when I advised him to participate as little as possible in the life of the Agency, because it seemed to have become so painful to him, to act dead in his office: "But I don't need to act, I already am – dead, that is...".

Sometimes, I find myself comparing him to a matt surface, with an infinite capacity to absorb, and reflecting only a tiny part of what it takes in. A bottomless well, never filled by the widest, the most contradictory reading sessions on the unsilvered mirror of his Sundays: from a string of crime novels to the writings of Li Tseu, via some learned work on the motifs in Oriental carpets, or the obscure Life of some minor Viennese Master.

Calling him one evening at home:
– Am I disturbing you? Were you having supper?
– Me, having supper? I "sup", as you put it, very rarely. No, I eat standing up, like a horse...

Behind the smooth, glabrous face, most often in repose, what eddies and whirlpools might there be, at times degenerating into some private, everyday carnage? What he once called, in a phrase that I found, though I never told him, somewhat mannered (but perhaps he was thinking less of himself than of the four walls of his office where we happened to be) "my little metamorphic theatre", meaning, undoubtedly, "changes for the worse". And yet, assuredly, on other days, what peace.

«Pour moi qui contrôle si peu ma vie et à qui beaucoup, dans l'existence, échappe, la ponctualité est tout ce qui me reste. Les premiers temps que j'étais ici, le concierge de l'immeuble prétendait qu'il pouvait régler sa montre sur mon passage: huit heures vingt, c'est l'heure à laquelle je traversais le hall et sortais de l'immeuble. Il me fallait environ vingt minutes pour me rendre à pied à l'Agence. Vers neuf heures moins vingt-cinq, j'arrivais devant une maison de retraite. C'était beaucoup plus qu'une maison, presque une petite ville avec chapelle privée, économat, jardins et grilles tout autour. Le bâtiment était immense, avec plusieurs ailes, une vraie gérontopole. En hiver, c'était parfois une vision de cauchemar, tous ces petits vieux qui avançaient à pas prudents dans le brouillard, la main crispée sur une canne ou s'appuyant sur leur tribune à roulettes, ou encore se tenant par le bras, deux par deux, par peur de la chute. Ils me faisaient penser à des petites veilleuses d'église, à la merci du moindre courant d'air un peu brusque. L'une des façades longeait la rue que je devais emprunter et il y avait toujours là, au troisième étage, une vieille dame qui me regardait passer. Elle avait pris l'habitude de me faire un petit signe de la main, auquel je répondais chaque fois. Elle était assise à une table bizarrement éclairée d'une mappemonde lumineuse, et sans doute en train de prendre son petit déjeuner. Un jour, je suis arrivé avec dix minutes de retard. Elle était là, à sa place habituelle, et a agité l'index comme pour, comment doit-on dire, me morigéner? Le manège a continué ainsi pendant près d'un an. Eh bien, l'hiver dernier, peu avant que je déménage pour la maison ensanglantée, j'ai constaté un matin qu'elle n'était pas à sa place. Ni le lendemain, ni les jours suivants. Puis ils ont remplacé les rideaux, et la disposition de la chambre a changé. Il était arrivé ce que tu devines. Mais elle a continué à me manquer lorsque je venais à pied le matin...»

. . .

"For someone like me, so little in control of my life and unable to grasp much of existence, punctuality is all I have left. When I first came here, my concierge claimed he could set his watch by my departure every morning: 8.20 was when I crossed the hall and left the building. It took me about twenty minutes to walk to the Agency. At around 8.35 I would pass a retirement home. It was much bigger than a house, more like a small town complete with private chapel, bursary, gardens and a surrounding fence. The building was huge, with several wings – a veritable gerontopolis. Sometimes, in winter, the vision was quite nightmarish, with all these little old people teetering cautiously through the fog, gripping their sticks or leaning on their zimmers, or else in pairs, arm in arm, for fear of falling. They made me think of those little votary candles in churches, at the mercy of the slightest gust. One of the buildings fronted on the street I had to take, and on its third floor was an elderly lady who always watched me go past. It was her habit to give a little wave, and I waved back each time. She would be seated at a table strangely lit by an illuminated globe, and was probably having her breakfast. One day, I arrived ten minutes late. There she was, in her usual place, and she wagged a finger, almost – how to put it – as if rebuking me? This arrangement continued for almost a year. Well, last winter, just before I moved to the blood-spattered house, I noticed one morning that she was not at her post. Nor the next day, nor the days that followed. Then they changed the curtains, and the room was rearranged. You can guess what had happened. But I used to miss her when I walked past every morning..."

. . .

Ou encore: «Tout ce qui dépassait, c'est-à-dire moi tout entier, ayant été progressivement rogné par les années, l'habitude et la nécessité, le sentiment de relief et de profondeur ne peut plus venir que des petits abîmes intérieurs. Qui ont, c'est vrai, cet avantage de pouvoir être sans fond. Car je sais par expérience que lorsque le volume de ce que je pense et ne dis pas excède, et de loin, la quantité de ce que je dis sans toujours le penser, c'est que l'équilibre intime est sérieusement menacé, compromis, devenu aussi friable que la colonne vertébrale d'une sardine en boîte...».

. . .

«Il faudrait que je fasse du sport. J'ai pensé à l'escrime. Qu'en penses-tu? J'aime bien l'idée d'être caché, protégé. Et offensif à la fois.»

Saxl a hérité de son grand-père un jeu d'échecs ancien, aux figures de bois polies, lustrées, qu'il déploie rarement sur les cases de l'échiquier pour empêcher que l'odeur (de cuir graissé, de tabac et, a-t-il fini par se persuader, «de champ de bataille prussien») ne s'en évapore à la longue et disparaisse tout à fait. De même m'avait-il une fois avoué éviter tout tête-à-tête prolongé avec untel, dont il a parfois du mal à supporter l'odeur aigrelette et ténue, mais tenace, de transpiration. «Ce n'est pas de ma faute si j'ai l'odorat très développé, beaucoup trop: une demi-heure après je peux encore te dire, sans risque de me tromper, lequel de mes collègues a pris l'ascenseur avant moi...». Une hyper-sensibilité qui lui fait parfois ressentir une goutte de pluie s'écrasant sur le dos de sa main avec la force d'un coup de marteau, une bouffée de vent frais comme un courant d'air glacé.

. . .

And again: "Now that everything beyond me, I mean my entire self, has been steadily whittled away by time, habit and necessity, the feeling of relief and depth can come only through small abyssal moments within. Which have, it's true, the advantage of being without substance. For I know from experience that when the volume of what I think and do not say exceeds, and by a long way, the volume of what I say without always thinking it, then my inner equilibrium is seriously threatened, compromised, and it becomes as brittle as the backbone of a tinned sardine…".

. . .

"I ought to take up a sport. I wondered about fencing. What do you think? I rather like the idea of being masked and protected. And at the same time, on the offensive."

Saxl inherited an antique chess set from his grandfather, with glossy, polished wooden pieces that he sets out only rarely on the board, in case the odour (of greased leather, tobacco and – he has managed to persuade himself – "of Prussian battlefield") should fade over time and vanish completely. In the same vein he once confessed that he avoided any prolonged tête-à-tête with X, because he sometimes found it hard to put up with the slightly bitter and muted, but nevertheless tenacious, body odour. "It's not my fault that I have a very – an overly – developed sense of smell: a half-hour later I can tell you exactly which of my colleagues has taken the lift before me …". It's a hyper-sensitivity that sometimes makes a drop of rain hitting the back of his hand feel like a hammer-blow, and a gust of cool wind as if it were an arctic draught.

. . .

«Non, ça ne va pas mieux … J'ai l'impression que tout continue de se détraquer un peu plus chaque jour. Ce matin, en me levant, j'ai regardé ma montre et, dans la petite lucarne qui indique la date, il m'a semblé voir exactement une minuscule fenêtre de prison, avec ses deux barreaux: le onze du mois … Et mes nuits ne valent guère mieux: la sensation d'un grand tronc couché sur la poitrine, et dont le poids finit par me réveiller. Sur quoi, à peu près satisfait de l'image et la trouvant assez juste, je me rendors plus tranquille … ».

. . .

«Parfois, en fin d'après-midi, lorsque le travail se relâche un peu, je regarde les murs du bureau autour de moi, puis le dernier soleil qui fiche le camp comme un petit morceau de braise posé sur les collines, et que la cendre des contours grignote peu à peu. Et ça dure, ça dure, comme une agonie … C'est en général le moment où je me dis que je fais sûrement fausse route depuis toutes ces années. Et qu'il n'est pas exclu, qu'il est même certain que je suivrai cette route-là, la fausse, jusqu'au bout. Puis j'attends encore un peu, le temps de ramasser mes affaires, de dire bonsoir à mon voisin s'il n'est pas déjà parti, et je rentre chez moi comme si de rien n'était. […]»

"No, I do not feel better ... I have the sense that every-thing is going more to pieces by the day. Getting up this morning I looked at my watch, and in the little square that shows the date, I seemed to see a tiny prison window with its two bars: the eleventh of the month ... And my nights are hardly better: the feeling that there's a great tree-trunk lying across my chest, whose weight finally wakes me. After which, more or less pleased with the accuracy of the image, I go to sleep again, somewhat calmer ...".

· · ·

"Sometimes at the end of the afternoon, when work lets up a bit, I look at the office walls around me, then the last of the sun disappears like a small ember laid on the hills, steadily nibbled away by their ashen contours. And it goes on, goes on, like an agony ... It's usually at that moment I tell myself I've surely been on the wrong track all these years. And that it's not impossible, it is in fact a certainty, that I shall follow this road, the wrong one, to the very end. Then I wait a while longer, the time it takes to gather my things, bid good evening to my neighbour if he has not already left, and go home as if nothing were wrong. [...]"

Sous le crible

(EXTRAITS)

Oublié sur la table de la cuisine, un flacon de collyre de marque Alcon, «Larmes naturelles II». On ne saurait mieux dire.

. . .

Des fraises des bois poussent sur le ballast, entre les traverses de la gare de l'Est. Un peu huileuses de goût et rachitiques de forme, mais il est donc possible de cueillir, en saison, des fraises sauvages dans le Xème arrondissement de Paris. Autre scène aperçue et ferroviaire, le repas de nourriture fraîche (insectes écrasés) prélevé par les moineaux sur les tampons de la motrice qui vient de s'immobiliser à quai: il faut les voir se maintenir quelques secondes à la verticale, en suspens, tels des colibris au-dessus d'une fleur exotique, exemple furtif d'une tentation qui pourrait être darwinienne.

. . .

Combien de temps loin de ce carnet, combien de semaines? Y voir le signe de l'immobilisation qui suit les retours, et dont je n'ai d'ailleurs aucune raison de me montrer autrement préoccupé. Ou la preuve que le quotidien retrouvé absorbe suffisamment, à défaut de contenter. L'occupation par les occupations, en quelque sorte. Reste la pensée en forme de liseron, celle qui grimpe et fleurit de part et d'autre de la voie tracée, du double rail des obligations: gratuite, désordonnée, parasite. Et envahissante. Pensée liseronne des carnets de route, de déroute. Jusqu'au prochain départ.

Under the Sieve

(EXTRACTS)

Left behind on the kitchen table, a bottle of Alcon eye-drops, "Natural Tears II". You couldn't put it better yourself.

.   .   .

Woodland strawberries grow on the gravel between the sleepers at the Gare de l'Est. A little oily to the taste, somewhat stunted in form, but wild strawberries, nonetheless, there for the picking, in season, in the 10th *arrondissement* of Paris. Another little railway vignette – the fresh meal (of crushed insects) that the sparrows pick off the buffers when the engine comes to a halt at the platform: the thing is to watch them hover upright for a few seconds, suspended like hummingbirds over an exotic flower – a fleeting instance of susceptibility, in the Darwinian sense.

.   .   .

How long since I last wrote in this notebook, how many weeks? I see this as a sign of the immobilization that follows upon my homecomings, though it ought not to worry me overmuch. Or maybe it proves that my old routine, once I get into it, is sufficiently absorbing, if not fulfilling. Being occupied with being occupied, so to speak. What's left over is thought, like bindweed – the type that climbs and flourishes here and there along the beaten path, along the rail-track of duties: free, chaotic, parasitical. And invasive. Bindweed-thought that fills the notebooks, ongoing, or going nowhere. Until I get away again.

A Reading List of Translations

No individual volumes of their work in translation exist for Henri Thomas, Paul de Roux and Gilles Ortlieb. These anthologies include selections:

Stephen Romer (ed.): *20th Century French Poems*, Faber, 2002 (includes de Roux, Ortlieb)

Mary Ann Caws (ed.): *The Yale Anthology of Twentieth-Century French Poetry*, Yale University Press, 2004 (includes de Roux)

Kevin Prufer and Wayne Miller, eds: *New European Poets*, Graywolf, 2008 (includes de Roux)

Jean Follain

D'Après Tout, trans. Heather McHugh, Princeton University Press, 1981

Transparence of the World: Selected Poems, trans. W. S. Merwin, Copper Canyon Press, 2003

130 Poems, trans. Christopher Middleton, Anvil Press, 2009

Philippe Jaccottet

Breathings, trans. Cid Corman, illustrated by Anne-Marie Jaccottet, Grossman, 1974

Seedtime, extracts from the notebooks 1954–1967, prose selections trans. André Lefevere, verse trans. Michael Hamburger, New Directions, 1977

Through an Orchard, trans. Mark Treharne, Aquila, 1978

Selected Poems, trans. Derek Mahon, Penguin Books and Viking, 1988

Cherry Tree / Le Cerisier, trans. Mark Treharne, Birmingham: Delos Press, 1991

Words in the Air, trans. Derek Mahon, Gallery Press, 1998

Landscapes with Absent Figures, trans. Mark Treharne, Delos
    Press/Menard Press, 1997
Under Clouded Skies with *Beauregard*, trans. Mark Treharne
    and David Constantine, Bloodaxe, 2000
Leçons / Learning, trans. Mark Treharne, Birmingham: Delos
    Press, 2001

Jacques Réda

The Ruins of Paris, trans. Mark Treharne, Reaktion Books,
    1996
Treading Lightly, Selected Poems 1961–1975, trans. Jennie
    Feldman, Anvil, 2005
Return to Calm, trans. Aaron Prevots, Host Publications, 2007

Guy Goffette

Charlestown Blues, Selected Poems, ed. and trans. Marilyn
    Hacker, The University of Chicago Press, 2007
Forever Nude, trans. Frank Wynne, Heinemann, 2008

Acknowledgements

For permission to include the original texts from the following books, we thank the poets and their publishers, to whom all rights are reserved:

Éditions Champ Vallon

GUY GOFFETTE: *Éloge pour une cuisine de province*, © Éditions Champ Vallon 1988

Éditions Claire Paulhan

HENRI THOMAS: *Carnets 1934–1948*, © Éditions Claire Paulhan 2008

Fata Morgana

JEAN FOLLAIN: *L'Épicerie de l'enfance*, © Fata Morgana 1999
JACQUES RÉDA: *Un voyage aux sources de la Seine*, © Jacques Réda and Fata Morgana 1987; *Moyens de transport*, © Jacques Réda and Fata Morgana 2000

Éditions Finitude

GILLES ORTLIEB: *Sous le crible*, © Éditions Finitude 2008

Éditions Gallimard

JEAN FOLLAIN: *Exister*, © Éditions Gallimard 1947; *Territoires*, © Éditions Gallimard 1953
GUY GOFFETTE: *La Vie promise*, © Éditions Gallimard 1991; *Partance et autres lieux*, © Éditions Gallimard 2000; *Un manteau de fortune*, © Éditions Gallimard 2001; *L'Adieu aux lisières*, © Éditions Gallimard 2007
PHILIPPE JACCOTTET: *Poésie 1946–1967*, © Éditions Gallimard 1971; *Paysages avec figures absentes*, © Éditions Gallimard 1976; *À la lumière d'hiver*, © Éditions Gallimard 1977; *Pensées sous les nuages*, © Éditions Gallimard 1983; *Cahier de verdure*, © Éditions Gallimard 1990; *Et, néanmoins*, © Éditions Gallimard 2001
GILLES ORTLIEB: *Place au cirque*, © Éditions Gallimard 2005
JACQUES RÉDA: *Amen*, © Éditions Gallimard 1968; *Récitatif,*

Le temps qu'il fait

For permission to include translations by the editors from works for which the following publishers hold English-language rights, we thank: Bloodaxe Books for Philippe Jaccottet's *Pensées sous les nuages*; Host Publications for Jacques Réda's *Retour au calme* and Reaktion Books for Jacques Réda's *Les Ruines de Paris*. Details of their editions are given in 'A Reading List of Translations'.